Treasures of the Heart

The Gifts of the Trinity

Kathy J. Smith

Treasures of the Heart

The Gifts of the Trinity

Kathy J. Smith

ISBN 978-1-61529-103-8
Copyright © 2011 by Kathy J. Smith

Revised 2022

Vision Publishing
P.O. Box 1680
Ramona, CA 92065
1-800-9-VISION
www.booksbyvision.org

All rights reserved worldwide.

No part of this book may be reproduced in any manner whatsoever without written permission of the author except brief quotations embodied in critical articles or reviews.

All scripture references are taken from the New American Standard Version of the Bible.

Acknowledgements

I would like to thank my parents Joe and Dorothy Smith for their undying love and dedication to see me through in the good times and the bad. I want to thank my children, Brett, Chad, Kristy, and Mindy, their spouses, and the eight blessings from God they have bestowed upon me.

Second, I want to thank my church family back in Ohio for their encouragement and support. Thanks to my friends Mickie and Rita for seeing me through some tough times and encouraging me when I needed a friend. Thanks to Bob and Barb Purkey for their loving support, and to Pastor Kerry Kirkwood for his words of encouragement.

I would also like to acknowledge and give a special thank you to Dr. Stan DeKoven and all the staff at Vision. Without their help, encouragement, and support, "Treasures of the Heart" would not have been possible. I am abundantly grateful for all that they have done and continue to do, as we endeavor to advance the Kingdom of God together. Thank you each one, you are such a blessing to me.

Last but certainly not the least, to the Lord Jesus Christ, to him be the glory.

This book is dedicated to:

Samantha

Delaney

Marenna

Gabrielle

Ricky

Connor

Ainslie

and

Tristan

They are treasures indeed,

in God's heart and mine.

Table of Contents

Acknowledgements 3
Author's Update 7
Foreword 9
Introduction 13
Unity is Power 15
Chapter One: Hidden Treasures 19
Chapter Two: The Gift of God 27
Chapter Three: Who are You? 33
Chapter Four: Who is <u>My</u> Father? 41
Chapter Five: What are Gifts? 49
Chapter Six: Which Member am I? 61
Chapter Seven: Gifts of the Son 71
    Five-Fold Ministry Gifts 72
    The Apostle 73
    The Prophet 75
    The Evangelist 77
    The Pastor 78
    The Teacher 79
Chapter Eight: The Gifts of Manifestation 89
    Word of Wisdom 92
    Word of Knowledge 93
    Discerning of Spirits 94
    Faith 96
    The Working of Miracles 97

Gifts of Healing 100
　　Prophesy 100
　　Diverse Kinds of Tongues 102
　　Interpretation of Tongues 102
Chapter Nine: Motivational Gifts 103
　　The Motivational Gift of Prophesy 110
　　The Motivational Gift of Serving 113
　　The Motivational Gift of Teaching 114
　　The Motivational Gift of Exhortation 116
　　The Motivational Gift of Giving 117
　　The Motivational Gift of Administration 119
　　The Motivational Gift of Mercy 120
Chapter Ten: Dry Bones to Glorified Bride 125
Closing Thoughts 133
About the Author 135

Author's Update

The original copy of this book was written in 2011, however much has changed since the original manuscript was written. Although God's word does not change, the world in which we live does. I do not think anyone could have predicted the magnitude of change we have experienced in the past few years. In addition, the revelation of God's word is always progressive. It is precept on precept, line upon line, according to the King James. (Isaiah 28:10) Therefore, an update was warranted.

This manuscript was revised in 2022 to include expanded material and a greater depth of understanding on the topic of spiritual gifts. It is also important to note that many highly respected scholars have written on this invaluable topic before me, biblical scholars like the renowned C. Peter Wagner. He addressed a total of twenty-seven different gifts in his teachings. Other notable authors such as Donald Gee, Leslie Flynn, and Rick Yohn to name just a few, have also written on the topic.

It would be difficult to deny the significance of C. Peter Wagner's work or the work of his contemporaries. They have each contributed invaluable input to the conversation on gifts. It would be challenging (if not impossible) to create an all-inclusive list of spiritual gifts. Everyone seemingly has an opinion, and what is considered a spiritual gift to one author may be considered a talent by another.

Alternatively, in this work I have chosen to focus on the gifts specifically mentioned by the Apostle Paul in Romans 12, 1 Corinthians 12, and Ephesians 4 and the three separate categories that they would suggest. This book attempts to build a biblical foundation upon which to begin exploring the different gifts and their function in the believer's life.

Based upon this biblical foundation, the purpose of spiritual gifts and how they are exercised will hopefully be realized, by the individual believer and the church alike. Discovering the gifts that God has hidden in your earthen vessel will help you to better understand the purpose for which you were created. Then you can find your place and utilize your gifts to advance God's kingdom. Spiritual gifts are the tools we use to do the work of the ministry and empower the church.

As I write this revision, I realize that more than any day before it is crucial that the church wake up, find her voice, and exercise her authority. Understanding your identity in Christ, discovering your gifts, and using them as God intended to benefit the body is your responsibility as a wise steward. We must each take responsibility to find our place and do our part to empower the church. This is arguably the most important day and hour in the history of the church, there is much at stake.

To God be the Glory,

Dr. Kathy Smith

Foreword

I was watching television the other night, watching the myriad of commercials related to my desperate need to eat. The umpteen thousands of calories they were laying out before my eyes were urging me to head to the fridge.

Thankfully, that night at least, my resistance was high. The hunger, which was not physical but psychological, felt so very real. I hungered for the junk that was presented through the images on the television; none of which I needed. They could not actually satisfy me, at least not the real me. The real me is Christ in me and the hope of glory.

Hunger and thirst are acknowledged as real forces in the word of God. We are told to hunger and thirst after righteousness, and we will be filled. Even the normal hunger that all people have in common will be filled because we serve a good God. Whether we serve him or not, he satisfies our need for food. Hunger is a universal experience.

In Jesus teachings, especially those emphasizing the Kingdom of God, there seemed to be an urgency or a hunger that he wished to create in the listener. For example, in Matthew 13:44 *"The kingdom of heaven (or Kingdom of God) is like a treasure hidden in the field, which a man found and hid again; and from joy over it he goes and sells all that he has and buys that field. Further, in verse 45 "Again, the kingdom of heaven is like a merchant seeking fine pearls, and in verse 46 upon finding one pearl of great value, he went and sold all that he had and bought it."* He sold it all, he went for it. He dug it out because it was priceless and worth every effort. He had to have it, so he laid it all down to obtain the one thing that mattered the most...the Kingdom of God.

In a similar way the book you have in your hands, written by my friend and colleague Kathy Smith, represents some serious desire and diligent digging. The desire of the writer, similar to the teaching of Christ, is to put a desire in the reader to read this book for all it is worth, and it is worth a lot. It is filled with precious jewels that can transform our lives.

The Gifts of the Trinity are found in every believer, but in order to possess the things we have been possessed for in Christ, there must be a desire in our hearts. We must be willing to pursue them although they are not far away. Holy Spirit lives within the believer. The gift of Holy Spirit, who possesses and distributes the gifts of the Father and the Son, is more than willing to see these gifts manifest in believers' lives...and we must want it. We must hunger for it, or at least become aware of it. It is that natural, spiritual hunger that we have within us to know the Lord more deeply, and to find out just what pleases Him (Eph. 5:10).

Secondly, we must also possess a diligence to dig out the precious gifts that the Lord has provided for us, as we daily labor in the word and worship. You might ask, "Why must we labor?" So that we can rest...but rest only comes to those who labor or enter the labor of the Lord. It is a bit difficult to grasp, but you will come to understand the concept fully when you search for it, out of the sincere desire to know the Lord more deeply. By diligently digging out the nuggets of truth found in God's word, and discussed in this book, the meaning will become clear.

The gifts of the Father, the Son and Holy Spirit are ours to have and enjoy although they are genuinely not for us. They are for the rest of the body of Christ "to profit withal." I hope you go for it! Get a burning hunger to know Christ better and diligently seek His gifts, especially to prophecy. As you hunger and thirst for His righteous gifts, you will indeed be blessed.

Stan DeKoven, Ph.D.

President Vision International University and VITEN

12

Introduction

There is rarely a day when a young woman is more beautiful than on her wedding day. For many, the preparations for this special day began months, perhaps even several years in advance of the blessed occasion.

Every single detail is set in place with great care to ensure the bride is perfectly adorned. The dress, the hair, the jewelry, the veil, the shoes, the make-up, even the flowers, everything must be exactly right for this once in a lifetime occasion. (At least we all hope it is a once in a lifetime occasion!)

Many different people become involved to ensure the success of the wedding and the following reception. There are the florists, the musicians, the vocalists, and the caterers. Then of course, there are the details of the wedding party to organize. Who will stand where and with whom? How will the whole wedding party get to the reception, then of course the pictures and the videos? Well, I could go on and on, but you get the point. I get tired just thinking about it!

There are so many details that must be attended to just to ensure that the day will be the glorious success that the bride and groom (well, at least the bride) have dreamed of. The plans and the people must be prepared and coordinated. The culmination of all this activity is the approach of the bride adorned in all her glory for her groom; they say their vows and exchange the rings, and finally there is the kiss.

One of the final rituals performed, although it is one of the most important parts of the ceremony, is the lighting of the unity candle.

The two candles representing the bride and groom's individual lives becoming unified and enlarged in the lighting of the one unity candle. Finally, they become one in Jesus Christ, making him the head of their house. Jesus is the third cord of the union that cannot be easily broken. Together in Christ, they stand in the strength and unity not equal to the sum of the two, but in the multiplied strength of a three-fold cord. Whatever the two of them agree upon, based upon the word of the Lord, will be done. The two of them together can achieve far greater things than either one of them could have achieved on their own.

"And if one can overpower him who is alone, two can resist him. A cord of three strands is not quickly torn apart."
Ecclesiastes 4:12

Unity is Power

"The glory which You have given Me I have given to them, that they may be one, just as We are one;"
John 17:22

The work of the church is to expand the Kingdom of God on the earth, and to equip and mature the saints so that the church might fulfill her role as the bride of Christ. This is done through the collaborative efforts of the gifts of the "Trinity." The gifts of the Trinity can be classified as three distinctive yet unified parts: Gifts of the Father (operational), Gifts of the Son (administrative), and Gifts of the Spirit (empowering). It is through the collaborative effort of the three distinct parts working together that the purpose of maturing the saints and preparing the bride might be completed.

For the sake of explanation, let us consider for a moment the work of a production facility as it produces its desired goal of a quality product.

The facility requires three separate but cooperative elements to complete its work. It requires an administrative staff to manage it, but the operations department produces the product. Then of course, there must be a source of power to fuel the work. The final product cannot be realized without the collaborative effort of all three. Let me give you an illustration, a ketchup factory in this case.

The raw material must go through certain operations or processing to become the finished product which is of course the ketchup. We all know that it does not start out as ketchup. It starts out as fresh, raw tomatoes. They are picked in the fields where they are grown and transported to the processing plant. There the tomatoes are placed on a conveyor where they are sorted and washed. Finally, they are cooked and prepared before becoming ketchup.

The whole process must be coordinated and managed by the staff to ensure that a quality product is achieved. Therefore, the owners of the ketchup factory must have an administrative department and an operations department to oversee the process. The work of turning tomatoes into ketchup is managed and supervised by the administration and operations crew and empowered with a source of fuel or energy to run the machines and equipment.

The effectiveness of the operation, and the quality of the final product, is dependent upon the operations department, the administrative department, and the source of energy. The three are <u>all</u> needed and must work effectively in conjunction with one another to create the final product.

What does this have to do with the preparation of the bride for Christ? Everything actually! No, we are not producing ketchup. What we are doing is starting with sinners, then leading them to Christ to become saved. Next, we disciple them; equipping them to work in unity with one another to create the final product. This final product is the perfected bride of Christ, adorned in all His glory. In other words, we see sinners transformed into saints.

So that the church can establish the kingdom and perfect the saints it requires the collaborative effort of all three gift sets. Collectively, we might refer to them as the gifts of the trinity. The gifts of the trinity consist of gifts of the Father, these are the motivational gifts (operational gifts); the gifts of the Son, which are the five-fold ministry gifts (administrative); and last but most certainly not the least are the gifts of the Spirit, known as the spiritual gifts (empowering).

What is the final product of the church? It is the bride of Christ. What is the raw product? The raw product is the sinner. Sinners must go through a series of operations (processed/transformed), to become perfected as saints. The saints must gather as one and then each member placed in their appropriate position to make up the body. The body must then be equipped to become the mighty army of God, ready for battle. Once the work is complete, we have a perfected body, the body of Christ... his bride.

Please refer my book, Power of Unity, *Empowered Believers Empower the Church* for more on this topic. [1]

---

[1] www.booksbyvision.org/product/the-power-of-unity/ The Power of Unity, *Empowered Believers Empower the Church* Vision Publishing by Kathy J. Smith

Chapter One:

Hidden Treasures

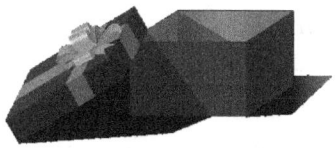

What have you invested in your children? What did God invest in you? As parents, we know that when we conceived our children a part of ourselves was invested into the future of that child. That child is an extension of ourselves, and not only did we contribute our own DNA for the formation of the child, but we also invested our time, our money, our energy, our hopes, and our dreams.

> **There is a treasure of immense value, a pearl of great price, and it is hidden in your vessel, do you love God enough to search for it?**

Matthew 13:44-52

Hidden Treasure "The kingdom of heaven is like a treasure hidden in the field, which a man found and hid again; and from joy over it he goes and sells all that he has and buys that field.

A Costly Pearl 45"Again, the kingdom of heaven is like a merchant seeking fine pearls, 46 and upon finding one pearl of great value, he went and sold all that he had and bought it."

A Dragnet 47"Again, the kingdom of heaven is like a dragnet cast into the sea, and gathering fish of every kind; 48 and when it was filled, they drew it up on the beach; and they sat down and gathered the good fish into containers, but the bad they threw away. 49 So it will be at the end of the age; the angels will come forth and take out the wicked from among the righteous, 50 and will throw them into the furnace of fire; in that place there will be weeping and gnashing of teeth.51 Have you understood all these things? They said to Him, 'Yes'. 52 And Jesus said to them, 'Therefore every scribe who has become a disciple of the kingdom of heaven is like a head of a household, who brings out of his treasure things new and old.'"

We are the treasure of God, the pearl of great price, hidden in the field. The treasure is hidden in earthen jars of clay.

"Therefore, I urge you, brothers, in view of God's mercy, to offer your bodies as living sacrifices, holy and pleasing to God--this is your spiritual act of worship." Romans 12:1

What do you treasure? Some treasure a rare coin collection, others like antiques. I have a watch that I treasure. It is unique because it belonged to my grandmother, and to her grandmother before her. I took it to a jeweler to have it appraised once. He told me it was worth truly little; the resale value was insignificant due to a missing hand.

The jeweler's low appraisal was insignificant in the end. It was the source of the watch that really mattered to me. Even though it had a low market value, I esteemed it as a treasure of great worth. Why? It was my legacy passed down from generation to generation and now invested in me.

It's not the watch that is important, but rather what the watch represents. It was entrusted to me for the future generations. It is my heritage which is more precious than gold. While some enjoy owning rare coins, stamps, and antique cars; it may not be the greatest treasure of their heart.

Some have a heart for missions; others have a heart for the lost. Still others cherish their Lazy Boy chair with a bowl of popcorn and a remote control nearby. How would you define the word treasure?

But we have this <u>treasure</u> in jars of clay to show that this all-surpassing power is from God and not from us. 2 Corinthians 4:7

We have <u>this</u> treasure. The treasure found in earthen vessels. The word treasure in the Greek is thesauros. When you study the origin of the word, it leads you to the word "deposit," it is a deposit or figuratively speaking, wealth. Deposited in our earthen vessel is a treasure from God.

It is the glory of God to conceal a matter, But the glory of kings is to search out a matter. Proverbs 25:2

If we want to discover the treasure God hid in our vessels, we will have to search it out.

God has made a deposit in your earthen vessel.

The word "deposit" is often used in reference to a financial investment such as in a checking or savings account. When I think of making a deposit, I remember my dad paying me an allowance each week.

One day he announced that he wanted to double the amount. I knew immediately, there had to be a catch. He then informed us that the second half of the allowance must be deposited in the bank.

He could have easily taken that same sum of money and placed it into a savings account on my behalf. It would have been far easier than convincing grade schoolchildren to save their allowance.

After all, the candy and toy isles of K-Mart were calling my name. In those days it was known as S.S. Kresge Corp., I know my age is showing. Despite my pleas to spend the whole sum of my allowance, he was relentless. Why? He wanted to instill in me the self-discipline of saving for another day. He wanted to teach me how to be a wise steward of my money.

Why was this so important to him? His own childhood was prematurely cut short when he had to drop out of school in the 7th grade to go to work and help to support his family. They moved constantly, often remaining in one place only a few months at a time. He worked hard to provide for his family, often working two jobs. His hopes and dreams of a better life for him and his children were evidenced by the investment of his time, money, and energy into our future.

At one time investing was considered a formidable vehicle for financial advancement. Unfortunately, in the days we live in the financial market has become less and less attractive each day. Savings accounts, stocks, and bonds can no longer offer the security they once provided.

Over the past few years many have lost substantial sums of money due to the decline in our global economy. Unemployment is at an all-time high. Many are struggling just to survive. Now more than ever, it is important that Christians know how to be wise stewards of all that they have been given. Jesus taught the principles of responsible stewardship in the parable of the talents.

Matthew 25:14 "For it is just like a man about to go on a journey, who called his own slaves and entrusted his possessions to them. 15 To one he gave five talents, to another, two, and to another, one, each according to his own ability; and he went on his journey.16 Immediately the one who had received the five talents went and traded with them and gained five more talents.17 In the same manner the one who had received the two talents gained two more. 18 But he who received the one talent went away and dug a hole in the ground and hid his master's money.19 Now after a long time the master of those slaves came and settled accounts with them.20The one who had received the five talents came up and brought five more talents, saying, 'Master, you entrusted five talents to me. See, I have gained five more talents.'21 His master said to him, 'Well done, good and faithful slave. You were faithful with a few things, I will put you in charge of many things; enter into the joy of your master.'22 Also the one who had received the two talents came up and said, 'Master, you entrusted two talents to me. See, I have gained two more talents.'23 His master said to him, 'Well done, good and faithful slave. You were faithful with a few things, I will put you in charge of many things; enter into the joy of your master.'24 And the one also who had received the one talent came up and said, 'Master, I knew you to be a hard man, reaping where you did not sow and gathering where you scattered no seed.25' And I was afraid, and went away and hid your talent in the ground. See, you have what is yours.'26 But his master answered and said to him, 'You wicked, lazy slave, you knew that I reap where I did not sow and gather where I scattered no seed.27' Then you ought to have put my money in the bank, and on my arrival I would have received my money back with interest.28'Therefore take away the talent from him, and give it to the one who has the ten talents.'29 For to everyone who has, more shall be given, and he will have an abundance; but from the one who does not have, even what he does have shall be taken away.30 Throw out the worthless slave into the outer darkness; in that place there will be weeping and gnashing of teeth."

What talents have been entrusted to you? What treasure has been deposited in your earthen vessel? Have you earned the title of wise steward? If not, it is not too late. It is important to manage all of God's investments in a profitable way.

Mum, won't you go on an adventure with me?

One day I was feeling a bit stressed. I had three grandchildren living with me at this time and I needed to get away for a few minutes of peace and quiet. I wanted to purchase some cleaning supplies so I thought it would be a great excuse to slip out for a little quiet time to myself.

I stepped into my office to gather my purse and phone when who would appear but the youngest of my grandchildren, Tristan. He had been challenging that day to say the least; wide-eyed with curiosity he watched as I gathered my things.

Finally, he spoke, his green eyes just beaming, his voice both gentle and innocent. He said, "Mum, would you go on an adventure with me?" Hmmmm The very child who had stressed me the most that morning was inviting me to go on an adventure. I could barely believe my ears, could this gorgeous little boy with the enticing voice be the same one who had been yelling and jumping on the furniture just moments before?

I hardly think a trip to the Dollar Store qualifies as an adventure, but it did to a three-year-old. How could I refuse such a sincere invitation? So much for a few quiet moments to myself! How <u>could</u> I resist? I could not. So, I looked for his coat and shoes and together we went on an adventure to buy cleaning supplies.

In similar fashion, life is an adventure. God wants to make the journey with you. Won't you allow him to take you by the hand, light your path, and lead you to your expected end in Him?

*"For where your treasure is,
There your heart will be also."
Matthew 6:21*

What do you treasure the most? I may not know what you treasure, but I can tell you what God treasures, God treasures you! He values you so much that he sent His Son to buy you back with his own blood. He has hidden his treasure in pots of clay and sent His Son to buy back the field where the treasure is hidden. Take time to discover the treasure God has invested in you.

Chapter Two:

The Gift of God

I have many fond childhood memories of growing up in rural northwest Ohio. The summer days usually consisted of hour after hour spent building sandcastles or swinging on the swing set in our backyard. When the borders of our property became too confining for our inquisitive little minds, my brother and I would meander into the field behind our home to begin our exploring.

The large mounds created by farmers cultivating the ground loomed ominous in the middle of the field behind our house. To my parents, they were little more than refuse piles of dirt, trees, and stone; but to two small children they were "hills" filled with untold treasures. Hills that beckoned us to come and discover their hidden secrets.

I understand arrowheads were frequently found in this area, but I remember finding little more than the wildlife. Wildlife such as rabbits, skunks, and snakes; as well as bugs and weeds! They were everywhere. Poison ivy and nettles were unsolicited bonuses to the scraped knees and elbows that we experienced while searching the hills for the illusive treasure.

There were no tangible treasures of value found in the "hills" of my childhood, but the satisfaction and the enjoyment my brother and I experienced along the way was a treasure indeed. How quickly the years have come and gone. So much has changed since the days of my youth. I am no longer a child, or even a young adult. My years of rearing a family are long since spent, only to see the cycle begin once again with my own children and grandchildren. So much has changed over the years, and yet some things are forever the same.

I no longer search for treasures buried in the earth of dirt mounds behind my house. No, those days have passed away with Howdy Dowdy, Rin Tin Tin, and Sky King. If you remember them your age is showing too!

Yet, my search continues, my search for hidden treasure. The treasure I now seek is one of tremendous value; it is a pearl of great price. Not gold or silver hidden in vessels of man's creation, but the treasure of God hidden in vessels of His creation, earthen vessels.

> Proverbs 25:2 *"It is the glory of God to conceal a matter, But the glory of kings is to search out a matter."*

Do you care enough to search for the treasure God hid in you? And what did this treasure in the earthen vessel cost? Who paid the price? Perhaps the songwriter Elvina Hall said it best in the hymn published back in 1879.

The chorus goes like this:

> ***"Jesus paid it all,***
> ***All to Him I owe;***
> ***Sin had left a crimson stain-***
> ***He washed it white as snow."***

Yes indeed, He did pay it all, and we owe it all to Him.

"I am going to be a church leader" announced four-year-old Ainslie."

As the instructor of a "Spiritual Growth Class," I found myself being asked some of the same questions repeatedly. "How can I discover my gifts" and "How can I know what God is calling me to do?"

One of my eight (now ten) grandchildren, our little four-year-old Ainslie had an especially important announcement to make one day. She said she knows what she is going to be when she grows up. She wants to be "a church leader." Actually…I thought she meant a cheerleader, but I was wrong. She quickly corrected me. Not a cheerleader mum, a church leader! Hmm, I thought to myself, what does a four-year-old know about becoming church leader? More than I had given her credit for obviously. When asked what she meant by "church leader" she responded with, "a pastor."

She added that she might like to be the praise and worship leader first, and then she will move on to being a pastor later. That is my Ainslie, she was a four-year-old with a powerful sense of purpose, vision and a long-range plan. I believe she has the stamina to make it too! A four-year-old with a purpose and a plan for her life; do you realize how many adults are still struggling to discover God's purpose and calling? What treasure has God hidden in your earthen vessel and how can you discover it?

Think of it this way. If you knew there was a ship loaded with treasure sunk in the sea, would you not go to the trouble of diving to obtain it? What about a treasure buried on a deserted island? If you knew where it was, would you not dig for it? I think most of us would agree, if we knew the location and we were certain there truly was a great treasure hidden at that site, it would be worth the effort and energy to search for it.

One day as I prayed, God gave me a vision of a room in Heaven where he eagerly awaits the visits of His children. The following account is my interpretation of what I saw, heard, and experienced there in His "Special Room."

I found myself approaching a huge white door, which is standing ajar. As I enter, my eyes immediately focus on the center of the room. There a male figure sits rocking in a tall white chair. As soon as he sees me enter, his eyes light up. I can tell by the smile on his face and the glint in his eye, He is pleased that I have come. "I was wondering when you would show up for a visit," He said. "Here sit down," as he motions to a soft furry rug under his feet. "Or pull up a chair if you prefer. Better yet, why not just come sit with me," and he motions for me to climb into his lap.

As I climb up, His warm arms wrap around me in a loving embrace. Several long minutes pass in complete silence. I am reluctant to move or speak, the tranquility and the joy I experience from being in His presence is breathtaking. Finally, He looks down at me with a warm fatherly gaze and asks, "How was your day?" Now I am aware that He knows precisely how my day has gone, nevertheless He listens intently. I begin by relating a dilemma I have been facing. He listens carefully doting on each word I say. Then he responds, "I'll tell you what we can do about that." He speaks to me, explaining step by step precisely what I should do.

A few more minutes passed, and I began surveying the surroundings in this "special room." Beside us is a table, and on it I see a book with my name engraved on the front. "Would you like me to read it to you?" he asks. As he opens the book and begins to read, I hear the story of how and why I was created.

Despite what anyone may have said, I was not a mistake. He talks to me about the many hopes, dreams, and visions he has for me. He explains that he had a specific purpose for forming me in my mother's womb. My birth was planned by God himself and he worked out each single detail in advance of my arrival. No, I was certainly not an accident. He had my end planned before the beginning.

I was so content just sitting there in his lap! But my visit was quickly ending, and I stood so that I could leave. It was then that my eye caught a glimpse of a huge pile of gifts over in a corner of the room. I had not seen them from the comfort of His lap, although how I missed them when I entered the room, I will never know.

They are wrapped in elegant paper and in a panorama of assorted colors and textures, each one tied with a huge frilly bow. His eyes follow mine to the corner where the gifts were stacked high and wide. "Those are the gifts that have not yet been opened. In fact, they haven't even been claimed.

I have these beautiful gifts, several for each one. I chose each person's gifts purposefully with the knowledge of what each would need to fulfill their call and purpose. Yet here they sit, unopened and collecting dust. It seems that for some it would be too much trouble, and it would take too much time, to discover and utilize the gifts I have given." You could feel his sadness in your innermost being, as his tears began to flow.

I felt saddened myself by his sorrow, so I hated to go. I found myself standing and gazing about the room for one last time. I paused trying to commit to memory each detail. I wanted to retain every ounce of the love, the joy, and the peace that I had experienced there. The glory of His presence filled the room to overflowing and the fragrance was breathtaking; like nothing else I had ever experienced before.

The overwhelming sense of tranquility that I felt made it difficult to leave. Yet I knew that I must. The unique work for which he created me is not yet complete. Reluctantly, I made my way to the door; my arms piled high with gifts. Now it is up to me to discover the gifts and the hidden treasures deep inside the boxes. It is up to me to utilize the gifts he has given. It is up to me to fulfill the call he has placed upon my life.

I found myself dedicated to the completion of my mission. I am more determined than ever to discover the gifts and the talents he has invested in my earthen vessel, the jar of clay. Even more importantly, I am determined to use those gifts as he intended for them to be used. They were intended to glorify him. After all, he wants to fill the whole earth with his glory, one vessel at a time.

I want to accomplish and fulfill the purpose for which he created me. I want to be <u>who</u> he called me to be, and to do <u>what</u> he has created me to do. I do not want to be as those that bring tears of sadness to his eyes. If he cries when he thinks about me, then I want the tears to be tears of sheer joy because I chose to glorify him.

Lord, please help each one of us fulfill your dream and vision for our lives. Help us accomplish the task for which you have created us, help us, O Lord, to glorify you. Amen

Chapter Three:

Who are You?

We talked earlier about what we as parents have invested in our child's future. We said, "The child is an extension of ourselves, and not only do we contribute our own DNA for the formation of the child, but we also invest our time, our money, our energy, our hopes and our dreams."

Now let me ask you this. What does God have invested in you as your spiritual father? Take a moment to just reflect upon that concept. If your earthly father contributed DNA to create you, what did your Heavenly Father contribute?

Genesis 1:26 "Then God said, "Let Us make man in Our image, according to Our likeness ; and let them rule over the fish of the sea and over the birds of the sky and over the cattle and over all the earth, and over every creeping thing that creeps on the earth." 27God created man in His own image, in the image of God He created him; male and female He created them."

We were made in the very image and likeness of God. What was it that he told Jeremiah in Jeremiah 1:5 ""Before I formed you in the womb I knew you, and before you were born, I consecrated you; I have appointed you a prophet to the nations."" He told Jeremiah he knew him even before he formed him. How could God know him before he existed in the flesh?

Even before he was conceived in his mother's womb he had already been conceived as a thought in the mind of God. Let me explain.

Our words are first formed in our mind as a thought, but once the thought is conceived in our mind it can then be released either orally or in written expression. A thought is merely a thought until it is expressed. Expression of a thought by faith then causes it to manifest. In other words, we were first created in the "mind" of God. We were first conceived as a thought and then spoken into being by Jesus Christ.

We, being the children of God, create in the very same fashion as our Heavenly Father. We first create through the power of thought. The scriptures tell us that we have the mind of Christ. This enables us to think and function as he did upon His Father's word and upon His word alone. Everything must be established upon the Word of God. Jesus said that he could do nothing unless he saw his Father doing it.

We cannot just speak our own fleshly desires into being. We must first think the thoughts of God, and then we speak and act upon what we see and hear our Father saying. We give that thought substance through faith, and then we speak it into being. The spoken word called the heavens, the earth, and all that there is into being, by the expression of the thoughts of God

Psalm 33:6 *"By the word of the LORD the heavens were made, And by the breath of His mouth all their host."*

Hebrews 11:3 *"By faith we understand that the worlds were prepared by the word of God, so that what is seen was not made out of things which are."*

1 Peter 1:23" *for you have been born again not of seed which is perishable but imperishable, that is, through the living and enduring word of God."*

All creation first began as a thought, and once expressed it was made manifest by faith.

In other words, spiritual conception precedes the act of physical conception in the creation of a human being. What did the Psalmist have to say?

Psalm 139:13 "For you formed my inward parts; you wove me in my mother's womb. 14 I will give thanks to you, for I am fearfully and wonderfully made; Wonderful are your works, and my soul knows it very well. 15 My frame was not hidden from You, When I was made in secret, And skillfully wrought in the depths of the earth; 16 Your eyes have seen my unformed substance; And in Your book were all written The days that were ordained for me, When as yet there was not one of them. 17 How precious also are your thoughts to me, O God! How vast is the sum of them! 18 If I should count them, they would outnumber the sand.

When I awake, I am still with you."

Uncovering the mystery of your DNA

This book is about the pearl of great price, the highly valued treasure hidden in you. It is about your spiritual heritage or you're "DNA." It is the spiritual investment of God himself hidden deep inside His earthen vessels. The potential of many in the body of Christ remains unclaimed and going to waste.

The gifts and callings of God are undiscovered. How can we discover the treasure of God? How can we know our calling, our gifts, and our purpose? "It is the glory of God to conceal a thing, but it the honor of kings to search it out. The purpose of this book is to help the members of the body of Christ know "the hope of His calling." Have you discovered who you were created to be?

I pray that the eyes of your heart may be enlightened, so that you will know what is the hope of his calling, what are the riches of the glory of His inheritance in the saints. Ephesians 1:18

What is DNA?

I was doing some research on the internet when I stumbled across this information about DNA. It said that scientists claim that the secret to who you are can be found in your DNA. So then, what is DNA? Where does it come from? DNA is the short form of the word deoxyribonucleic acid. That is a mouth full!

Do you realize that the human body has some 50 to 75 trillion cells? Inside the nucleus of each cell are two long strands of DNA that have been twisted into a double helix. When the cell is at rest these strands lie about loosely, but when it gets ready to reproduce itself, it condenses into a tight compact unit which is then known as a chromosome. When the DNA is found in specific patterns it can also be referred to as genes.

Remember DNA is the instruction manual, the blueprint of an organism. Each DNA molecule consists of millions of protein molecules which are organized into 30,000 genes. The strands of DNA are made up of ribbons of deoxyribonucleic acid that appear in the form of a ladder.

The sides of the ladder are made up of four basic proteins. It is the specific combination of these proteins and how they are arranged that will determine the structure and the function of every living cell inside the human body.

DNA is the encapsulated potential of your expected end.

Your DNA encodes your potential height, weight, body structure, and your eye and hair color directly into your genes. Who you are and who you can become are all mapped out ahead of time the moment you were conceived. Your potential is predetermined by your DNA. What you make of that potential is up to you.

An athlete takes his physical strengths and abilities and focuses on his potential by training and diligence. But to be successful, he must be dedicated to giving 100% to the preparation of his mind, will, and body for the event in which he wishes to compete. Those who are not fully committed will never reach their fullest potential.

Jeremiah 29:11 *"'For I know the plans that I have for you,' declares the LORD, 'plans for welfare and not for calamity to give you a future and a hope."* The KJV says "to give you an expected end."

What thoughts was God thinking when he created you? What is your expected end? What is your hope and future in Him? If you will, indulge me in a few moments of poetic expression in the explanation below.

God wants to remove the scales from the eyes of our hearts. He wants to clarify our vision. He wants to enlighten us to know who we are and who we are to become. God wants to give us the knowledge that empowers us to become and do His will.

Hope is given assurance (substance in KJV) by faith. (See Hebrews 11:1) It is the homing beacon of our spirit lighting the path to our expected end. The vision of our expected end becomes sharper and more focused as our spiritual eyes become increasingly more enlightened to the revelatory truth in God's word. We learn little by little, line upon line and precept on precept.

Have you ever tried to look through a microscope or camera lens before it is focused? It is difficult or perhaps even impossible to make out the object you are trying to view. As one begins to adjust the focus of the lens, the vague blobs begin to take shape and emerge. With the help of even greater magnification, even the minutest of details will begin to avail themselves for our viewing.

Our hope is the dreams and desires of our heart being birthed by love and given substance by faith. The very dreams and desires God intended us to have when he created us. It is our spiritual DNA. The vision of that calling reveals our purpose, our expected end, our destiny in Christ. The vision is made clear by the revelation of the intents and purposes of God. It is the Holy Spirit that acts as the microscope to focus in on that truth and make it clear to our spiritual eye.

Hebrews 6:18-19 *"so that by two unchangeable things in which it is impossible for God to lie, we who have taken refuge would have strong encouragement to take hold of the hope set before us. 19 This hope that we have as an anchor of the soul, a hope both sure and steadfast and one which enters within the veil."*

What is it but hope that keeps us from being swept away by the storms of life and keeps us afloat, as the anchor of our souls? What is it that is left when all else has failed unless it be hope?

Romans 8:24-25 *"For in hope we have been saved, but hope that is seen is not hope; for who hopes for what he already sees? 25 But if we hope for what we do not see, with perseverance we wait eagerly for it."*

Not only do we need faith to please God, but we also need faith to see our hopes fulfilled.

Dreams and desires give birth to hope. But it is faith that gives hope substance.

Hebrews 11:1, *"Now faith is the assurance of things hoped for, the conviction of things not seen."* Each of us is given a measure of faith and it is that faith that gives our hope substance. How?

Galatians 5:6 *"For in Christ Jesus neither circumcision nor uncircumcision means anything, but faith working through love."*

So, if it is faith that gives our hopes and dreams substance, then it is love that acts as a catalyst to our faith to make it manifest. Our hopes and dreams are given substance by faith and activated by love. If faith were the flour in your bread dough, then love is the yeast that makes it rise.

If I were to ask you what a cake is made of you may answer flour, sugar, and eggs. Just as cake is not a cake until you put all the ingredients together and allow it to bake; a dream is not a reality until it is conceived in hope, given substance by faith, and birthed in love.

Matthew 13:44-46 *"The kingdom of heaven is like a treasure hidden in the field, which a man found and hid again; and from joy over it he goes and sells all that he has and buys that field."*

Isn't it time to unearth the treasure of God in your vessel? Isn't it time to invest the wealth of God with which you have been entrusted? Isn't it time that the blessings of God become manifest within your life? Jesus paid the price to buy back the field with the hidden treasure, the treasure of God hidden in your vessel. Don't allow his sacrifice to go to waste.

1 Peter 1:18-23 *"knowing that you were not redeemed with perishable things like silver or gold from your futile way of life inherited from your forefathers, 19 but with precious blood, as of a lamb unblemished and spotless, the blood of Christ. 20 For He was foreknown before the foundation of the world, but has appeared in these last times for the sake of you 21 who through Him are believers in God, who raised Him from the dead and gave Him glory, so that your faith and hope are in God. 22 Since you have in obedience to the truth purified your souls for a sincere love of the brethren, fervently love one another from the heart, 23 for you have been born again not of seed which is perishable but imperishable, that is, through the living and enduring word of God."*

Who are you in Christ? It is not who your friends say that you are, it is not who you family members say that you are, but who God says you are. Who does God say that you are? God alone knows your potential, trust him to guide you to discover all of who you were created to be….

Lord, enlighten the eyes of my heart that I might know the hope of your calling and the riches of the glory of your inheritance in the saints. Amen (See Ephesians 1:18)

Chapter Four:

Who is <u>My</u> Father?

Who one's father is can be extremely important! It was vitally important in Jesus' day. People, especially in Jesus' day, identified a person by their family name, if the father had a good reputation, then so will the son. People will credit you with a certain integrity or lack of it based merely upon one's name. You don't have to earn it; it is freely given like one's inheritance. A family name can be highly important. People want to know where they came from.

Many of those adopted at birth have spent endless amounts of time, energy, and money searching for their biological parents. Having a good relationship with one's parents can be extremely helpful in the development of an individual's sense of self-identity. Great insight into one's personal make-up can be gained through the understanding of who an individual's parents are.

Many search their family bloodline to discover the secret to who they are and where they came from. The search for a personal genetic history has captivated the minds of many. If the knowledge of our biological ancestry is of such grave importance, then how much more significant is the search for our spiritual heritage? What are your spiritual roots and where did you come from? Do you know your spiritual father? Do you have a good relationship with him? Having a personal relationship with the Father means that we spend time getting to know him and His nature.

Ultimately, God is our spiritual Father. He is the one who created us. In Genesis 1 we read that God said, "Let us make man in our image...." The "our" is a plural personal pronoun referring to the Godhead; God the Father, God the Son, and God the Holy Spirit. God is one God, but he is a triune God being three persons in one. Three is often referred to as the number of divine perfection.

Each member does not in and of himself bring completion to the Godhead, but the three functioning together do. Each individual member is complete within himself, and has his own unique attributes, gifts, abilities, and personality. Each one brings to the table qualities that compliment and support the others... To better understand the triune God, let us first examine the makeup of a triune man.

1 Thessalonians 5:23 *"Now may the God of peace Himself sanctify you entirely; and may your spirit and soul and body be preserved complete, without blame at the coming of our Lord Jesus Christ."*

Man is a triune being made in the image and likeness of God. He is a spirit which has a soul, housed within a body. That is right, just as our Father is a triune being, so are we. We are one human being, but we consist of three parts. The three parts of man are our spirit, soul, and body. God first created the physical body, then he breathed into him the breath of life and the combination of the three together created the soul. The soul is created by the union of the spirit of man and his physical body. (Man became a living soul.)

The spirit of God and the spirit of man are not one in the same, (see Romans 8:16 and Genesis 2:7 as well as the diagram below.) The soul equates to self-consciousness while the Spirit equates to our God consciousness. The soul is made up of our mind, our will, and our emotions. The Spirit provides to us communion with God, an intuition, and a conscience.

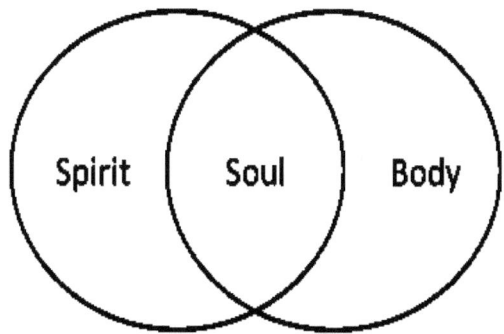

Before the fall, Adam lived in perfect harmony with God (or so we assume). Remember man is made of three parts: spirit, soul, and body. The soul, which is man's mind, will, and emotion humbled itself to the direction of the spirit of God. His spirit was in complete communion with the Spirit of God. Therefore, man was able to walk in complete harmony with the spirit of God because he was in direct and daily communion with God's spirit.

Our spirits are unable to have communion with God until we have been born again. Why? As the result of Adam's fall each of us was born into sin. Unsaved people do occasionally have answers to prayer and sometimes hear from God, but they cannot have a meaningful personal relationship with him until they are born again. Sin acts as a barrier or a veil preventing us from seeing truth. Once we become of an accountable age, we are responsible for seeking the truth on our own.

The enemy wants to keep the veil over our eyes; he does not want us to know who we really are and who he really is. Once we understand, we can then take our rightful place in authority over him. He does not want that to happen, so he tries to keep us in the dark about our identity and our authority in Christ.

It is the sinful nature of mankind that has blinded the eyes of the unbeliever. Once we accept Jesus Christ as our Lord and Savior, allowing him to pay our sin debt, we can then stand in a right relationship with God. His blood washes away the sin, the veil is removed from our eyes, and the process of renewing our mind begins. Then is the communication of our spirit with His spirit renewed as well.

Why must we have our mind renewed? Why isn't merely a salvation experience enough? Just as a newborn baby sees only faint shadows at first, so we can only see very dimly. A baby Christian will recognize Christ as their Savior and redeemer just as the newborn infant knows and senses his mother. Nevertheless, the newborn is unable to communicate in the way an adult does. As Jesus stated to Nicodemus, one must be "born again" to simply see the Kingdom of God, let alone entering its fullness. (John 3)

A newborn expresses his needs through body language and crying. He cannot tell you his name, chew whole food, or drive the car. Those things come after the mind and body have had the opportunity to gain experience and develop from the proper nutrition. They cannot walk until they have mastered the control of their muscles and strengthened them over the course of time by using them.

Yes, when we accept Jesus as our Savior, we do know who our Father is; we know who our brother is. Ask a newborn Christian to explain to you what the different covenants are and how they affect our Christian walk, and they will look at you as though you were speaking Chinese. They need time to renew their minds before we can expect them to comprehend the deeper thoughts and ways of God. It is a process that is accomplished gradually through time spent in prayer, God's presence, and in His word; we learn to exercise our faith by reason of use.

John 4:24, *"God is spirit, and those who worship Him must worship in spirit and truth."*

There are two kinds of bodies,

Celestial and terrestrial.

1 Corinthians 15:41 *"There is one glory of the sun, and another glory of the moon, and another glory of the stars; for star differs from star in glory. 42 So also is the resurrection of the dead. It is sown a perishable body, it is raised an imperishable body; 43 it is sown in dishonor, it is raised in glory; it is sown in weakness, it is raised in power; 44 it is sown a natural body, it is raised a spiritual body. If there is a natural body, there is also a spiritual body. 45 So also it is written, 'The first MAN, Adam, BECAME A LIVING SOUL.' The last Adam became a life-giving spirit. 46 However, the spiritual is not first, but the natural; then the spiritual. 47 The first man is from the earth, earthy; the second man is from heaven. 48 As is the earthy, so also are those who are earthy; and as is the heavenly, so also are those who are heavenly. 49 Just as we have borne the image of the earthy, we will also bear the image of the heavenly."*

We being human have a natural body, but God is a spirit and has a spiritual body. He has a mind, will, and emotions even as we do. He is therefore a person or rather <u>three</u> persons, Father, Son, and Holy Ghost.

God the Father

We know our Heavenly Father through the teachings of Jesus Christ and the revelation given to us by Holy Spirit. Jesus said in John 14:7 *"If ye had known me, ye should have known my Father also: and from henceforth ye know him, and have seen him."*

We know him as he has revealed himself to us in the scriptures. We know him as he reveals himself to us by reason of our own intimate personal relationship with him. He is our refuge, our protector, our provider, our shield, and our buckler. We know that he is omnipresent, omnipotent, and holy. He is merciful and just. He is righteous. God is all these things and more. He is also the father of our Lord Jesus Christ.

God the Son

We see predictions of Christ's birth throughout the Old Testament, but finally in the New Testament we see a record of his birth and life here on earth. John records that in the beginning was the Word and the Word was with God and the Word was God. (See John 1) Although they are one in unity, they are separate in personhood. Jesus is the only Son that is begotten of the Father. Jesus could do nothing unless he saw his Father do it. He prayed to his Father and did the will of his Father and returned to sit at the right hand of the Father. They are one, yet they are separate.

Jesus is the first of many and each one of us that accepts him becomes a joint heir with him and is seated with him in Heavenly places. It was Jesus the Son, not God the Father that died on the cross that day, and then rose again. It was Jesus that paid the debt we could not pay. Jesus is our redeemer; He is our Lord and our Savior; he is the one who continues to intercede for us in Heaven.

Jesus promised not to leave us comfortless, but before he ascended, he instructed the disciples to tarry until they had been endued with power from on High. Jesus is the one who came to establish the Kingdom and commissioned us to do the same.

God the Holy Spirit

It is Holy Spirit that leads us into all truth. He baptizes believers into the body of Christ. He imparts the love of the Father and helps us to pray. He is the teacher. He knows the things of God and brings all things pertaining to God to our remembrance. He corrects men of sin. He is a witness of the sonship of Jesus Christ. He speaks the word of God through men and writes on the fleshly tablets of man's heart making us the living epistles of Christ.

He is sent of God and Jesus Christ to comfort God's people. He gives life and liberty and transforms men into the image and the character of God. He helps us to both know and obey the truth and strengthens the inner man. He fills men with the Spirit giving gifts for the work of the ministry. He is equal to God the Father and God the Son. He is the third person of the Godhead.

Each member of the Godhead has distinctive characteristics and work that makes them unique. Each has different gifts to impart to individual believers and the church. For instance, Holy Spirit has spiritual gifts to impart into individual believers empowering them for the work of the ministry. He divides them and distributes them as he wills to each one.

For further study on the Trinity please refer to Dr. Stan DeKoven's book, "New Beginnings."[2]

---

[2] "New Beginnings: A Sure Foundation" by Dr. Stan DeKoven, Vision Publishing.

Chapter Five:

What are Gifts?

"Now concerning spiritual gifts, brethren, I do not want you to be unaware." Paul said in 1 Corinthians 12:1 that he did not want us to be ignorant concerning the gifts. So why did he find it so important that we understand the gifts? Our gifts help to define who we are.

Take Joseph the biological father of Jesus for instance, who did people say that he was? He was Joseph the carpenter. His gift for working with wood gave him an occupation and his identity was tied to his occupation and gift.

What could be more crippling to the development of an individual than to rob him of the knowledge of who he is? I hear the words of this scripture resonating in my spiritual ears, "My people perish for lack of knowledge!" Satan has blinded the eyes of generations of believers. He has been hiding the truth of <u>who</u> we are in Christ and <u>who</u> we have been called to become.

He desires to weaken the effectiveness of our ministries by trying to rob us of our own spiritual identities. What could be more fundamental to our development than the knowledge of who we are?

I recall a story related to me once about a woman who lost all that she owned. She was reduced to living in the streets and eating the food she could find in the dumpsters. It was a very sad story of a woman whose family had owned the biggest business establishment in town. Times got rough and finally the business went under. Eventually all her family died, and she was left to herself. Finally, she too died a pauper with no home.

When they prepared her for her burial, they discovered a pendant hung around her neck. It was a very unusual looking stone, so it was taken to the local jeweler for appraisal. No one anticipated what happened next, it was worth millions of dollars.

The treasure was useless to her now. Unfortunately, she had failed to recognize the value and importance of the stone while she was still alive. She was homeless, a destitute person, needlessly dying as a pauper. She was unaware of the treasure she held in her possession. That lack of knowledge caused her to perish in the streets instead of in the lovely home she could have afforded.

Knowledge is power.

God's people are perishing for the lack of knowledge. The treasure of God in earthen vessels often goes unclaimed. Do you know the treasure of God hidden in your vessel? Did you realize that he has given us the power to create wealth? He did not give us wealth; he gave us the power to create it.

Most Christians are familiar with the gifts of the Spirit. Many also know about the five-fold ministry gifts. An abundance of teaching is available on either subject. A third set of gifts has had far less prominence in the Christian educational arena. The gifts that I speak of are the motivational gifts which have been given to us by our Heavenly Father.

What is a Motivational Gift?

We were each born with a personality or lifestyle gift. It is a gift of grace. It is not something we have earned. It is fundamental to who we are in Christ Jesus and who we were called to be. If we are to be fully effective in the work to which we have been called, then we must first and foremost come to the knowledge of the truth of who he created us to be.

Let us examine this scripture.

Romans 12:6-8 *Since we have gifts that differ according to the grace given to us, each of us is to exercise them accordingly: if prophecy, according to the proportion of his faith; 7 if service, in his serving; or he who teaches, in his teaching; 8 or he who exhorts, in his exhortation; he who gives, with liberality; he who leads, with diligence; he who shows mercy, with cheerfulness. NAS*

We have each been graced with a gift from our Heavenly Father. There are a total of seven motivational gifts that in totality represent the person and work of our Lord Jesus Christ. The gifts, all seven of them were evident in the life of Christ but each of us has received a measure of that gift of God. (See Ephesians 4:7) We should have evidence of all seven gifts in our lives, but one gift is most dominant in each of us.

For clarity let me repeat, Jesus had all seven gifts in the fullness of each one, we do not. We have a portion of all seven gifts but not the fullness. We have one gift in more abundance than the others, that one gift would be considered our dominant motivational gift.

This is why we need each other; it is when the individual members of the body of Christ unite that the body can realize the fullness of all the gifts operating together. We are individual members of one body. Just as the foot is not the body, and the hand is not the body, but the body is all the members together. The body is less effective when one part is missing.

Can you imagine trying to walk without a foot or leg? Can you imagine trying to see without your eyes? All members are needed to complete the body and to function appropriately. "We have gifts" ... which is the word "*Charismata*" in the plural form of the Greek and the singular form is a word familiar to many of us, "*charisma*."

> **Let us examine the root meanings of this word in the Greek.**
> 1. *chara* = joy
> 2. *charis* = grace in the abstract
> 3. *charisma* = grace made available in a specific and personal way empowering the one that possesses it.

When we recognize our gift of grace and minister through that gift, we will <u>minister with joy</u>. (*chara*) A sense of fulfillment and satisfaction that can only be fully realized as we learn to function in our place within the gift of grace that God has given to us.

The gift is defined as a "spiritual endowment", a gift of grace. The gift is a lifestyle or personality gift. It is not something that can be earned. Just as there are varieties of gifts there are also varieties of ministries and varieties of effects. We each have the one gift, the motivational gift with which to minister to one another in the body.

> "As each one has received a special gift, employ it in serving one another as good stewards of the manifold grace of God." 1 Peter 4:10

The motivational gift is that gift which motivates us to act in the way that God had intended, to enable us to fulfill our purpose. It energizes us, thus we get the word "motivate." It is the special endowment of grace or grace gift that makes it possible to do that for which we were created.

Motivation can come in several different forms. Think about your child or pet for instance. What motivates them to act in the way that they do? My grandson acts almost hysterical any time a spider, fly, ant, or any insect is seen near him. He is deathly afraid of anything like that, so his fear causes him to react with panic. Fear is one type of motivation.

We may use a form of reward or incentive to motivate our children to do what we want. Promises of candy, gifts, money, and so on are used to prompt them to respond in the way that we feel is beneficial. For instance, we may offer an allowance if all chores are done consistently for one week. We may allow them to earn special privileges for good grades. All are forms of motivation.

Another form of motivation is simply our own personalities. Our inborn personalities may cause us to act shy, confrontational, outgoing, competitively, etc. It is the gift of who we are, and it motivates us to act in a specific manner. Paul outlines seven different motivational gifts for us in Romans 12:6-8.

We will study each of these gifts in detail in the coming chapters, but for the purpose of introduction, this is a list of the motivational (grace) gifts as found in this scripture:

> 1. **Prophesy/Perceiving**
> 2. **Serving**
> 3. **Teaching**
> 4. **Exhorting**
> 5. **Giving**
> 6. **Ruling or Administration**
> 7. **Mercy**

We are to use the gift of God to bring unity to the body. He created us with this motivational or lifestyle gift so that we could more effectively do the work of the ministry and meet the needs of the body.

Paul outlines 3 categories of gifts in the scripture below.

1 Corinthians 12:4-6 "Now there are varieties of gifts, but the same Spirit. 5 And there are varieties of ministries, and the same Lord. 6 There are varieties of effects, but the same God who works all things in all persons."

1. *Gifts of the Holy Spirit in verse 4.*
2. *Gifts of the Son in verse 5.*
3. *Gifts of the Father in verse 6.*

We have discussed the gifts of the Father listed in verse six already, but what about the other two sets of gifts? Verse four mentions the gifts of the Holy Spirit. These gifts are the nine spiritual gifts given by "Holy Spirit" as He wishes to provide us with the power to minister

Look at the scriptures below:

1 Tim. 4:14 *"Do not neglect the spiritual gift within you, which was bestowed on you through prophetic utterance with the laying on of hands by the presbytery."*

2 Tim. 1:6 *"For this reason I remind you to kindle afresh the gift of God which is in you through the laying on of my hands."*

Paul was reminding Timothy of his responsibility to use the gift that God had given to him. It was not for Timothy to keep to himself. It was given to edify and care for the body. Just as we saw earlier in the parable of the talents, it is up to each of us to use the gift wisely as good stewards of that which was entrusted to us by our Father.

I want to remind you of the example that we used in the beginning. The example of the ketchup factory and the three groups or departments needed to make it function effectively. An administrative department, an operations department, but also a source of power was needed. The Holy Spirit empowers the individual believer to do their ministry.

The gifts of the Holy Spirit consist of three groups of three gifts. We will define them more thoroughly in the coming chapters, but this list will serve to remind you of the gifts given by the Holy Spirit. We are not limited to one but are instructed to desire the best gifts. Which gift is the best? The one that most meets your need at the time that you need it of course.

Revelatory Gifts	Power Gifts	Vocal Gifts
Word of Wisdom	Faith	Tongues
Word of Knowledge	Miracles	Prophesy
Discerning of Spirits	Gifts of Healing	Interpretation of tongues

Finally, we have the gifts of the son or the five-fold ministry gifts. These gifts are often referred to as the working part or hand of God upon the earth. When one refers to the five-fold ministry the five fingers on the hand can be utilized to help the student remember the different ministry gifts and their purpose in the body.

1. The thumb is said to be the apostle. It touches every other ministry.
2. The forefinger is the prophet for he can point things out that others may not see, pointing to the past, present, and future.
3. The third finger is the longest and reaches the farthest. This represents the ministry of the evangelist.
4. The fourth finger is the ring finger and stands for the pastor. The pastor can connect the flock with the heart of God.
5. And finally, we have the little finger that represents the work of the teacher. They can probe into areas that others cannot.

The purpose of the five –fold ministry is to lead, guide, and direct the individual believers in the body of Christ through the ministry given to them. They are to assist the newborn in Christ to grow, mature, and find their place in the body. They are to set them in their proper place so that the whole body can benefit from their gift and ministry. They are to equip them and the other believers in the body for the work of the ministry.

The collaborative efforts of all gifts in the three classifications help to bring unity to the body as a whole. This is evidenced by the three primary scriptural texts that reveal the working of the gifts. First, in 1 Corinthians 12:8-10 the scripture that unveils the listing of the spiritual gifts, is preceded by the verse explaining that the gifts are for all to prosper, not just the one possessing the gift. The gift is for the benefit of the whole body.

Then in verse twelve we see the explanation of how the whole body is one but many different but significant members. If we look back to what Paul was talking about just prior to the listing and teaching on the gifts, we can find a plea for unity in the serving of the Lord's Supper.

Once again in the scripture reference found in Romans twelve that lists the motivational gifts, we see Paul emphasizing unity. In verse five and six he calls to their attention that they are made up of many members but are all one body and members of one another. He ends the teaching on gifts with one last admonishment to love one another, to favor one another and to have the same focus of purpose. Unity is again the focus in and around the teachings on the gifts. (Refer to *Power of Unity* for more on this.)[3]

---

[3] www.booksbyvision.org/product/the-power-of-unity/ The Power of Unity, *Empowered Believers Empower the Church* Vision Publishing by Kathy J. Smith

Finally in Ephesians 4:11 we have the teaching on the five-fold ministry. The whole teaching focuses upon bringing the body into unity with itself in love. He explains that each part or member, when it works effectively and in its rightful place, causes the body to grow and mature into the fullness of Christ.

We have three separate but unified members of the Godhead giving gifts to the body that in turn work together to build and mature the body of Christ. The gifts of the Father, which are the functional or lifestyle gifts give us identity and personality, they motivate us to do what we are called to do. These are the gifts of grace for they are neither earned nor chosen, they are freely and intentionally given by our heavenly Father.

The gifts of the five-fold ministry equip the body to function together in maturity like a well-oiled machine. Finally, we have the gifts of the Spirit that empower the body to function supernaturally. They are the tools we use to minister to one another.

Without all three gift sets the work of maturing the church, the bride of Christ, by turning sinners into saints could not be accomplished. Just as the Godhead would not be complete without all three members, the body cannot work effectively without all three sets of gifts working in harmony and in conjunction with one another bringing about unity with maturity. Thus, we see how the prayer of Jesus is to be completed; he prayed that we might all become one, even as they (the Godhead) are one.

"The glory which You have given Me I have given to them, that they may be one, just as We are one;" John 17:22

Some would say we are already one in Christ, and technically we are. We are already a part of His body. However, just because we are already members of His body it does not mean that we are all working together in harmony and maturity. One could put five toddlers in the same room together but that does not mean they can work together as a team to accomplish a specific task. That type of cooperation and unity requires maturity that they do not yet possess. A mature church makes unity possible.

"...Behold, how good and how pleasant it is For brothers to live together in unity!" Psalms 133:1b

Chapter Six:

Which Member am I?

1 Corinthians 12:4 "Now there are varieties of gifts, but the same Spirit. 5 And there are varieties of ministries, and the same Lord. 6 There are varieties of effects, but the same God who works all things in all persons. 7 But to each one is given the manifestation of the Spirit for the common good."

Let us examine this scripture more closely. We see the words varieties and all or the same repeated several times. There are varieties of different gifts, ministries, and operations but they all work together. Just as there are different gifts, there are also different members of the body that are to work together as one.

The gifts of the trinity work together in a specific order, as can be evidenced in the scripture above with the Holy Spirit in verse four always focusing on and revealing the son, as is seen in verse five. In a similar manner, The Son is always focused on revealing the Father, as is seen in verse six.

Finally, in verse seven the Father's will and purpose is revealed in an open demonstration (manifestation). They work together through a coordinated effort using their gifts to benefit the church and advance God's kingdom. This is how we coined the phrase, "Gifts of the Trinity."

Just as the Godhead is made up of three persons functioning together as one; so are we, the body, made up of many members functioning as one body. In the twelfth verse of that same chapter

Paul discusses the many members making up the one body. He states that all the members are not one in the same.

If you tried to write with your foot, it would be extremely difficult. If you tried to walk on your hands, that too would be equally as difficult because your hands were not meant to carry your body weight, your feet were. Things work best when we use the proper body part for the job it was intended to do. The part must be in the proper place and not displaced in the body.

The members of the church body can function at optimum level when we allow the proper member to accomplish each task. Try using your elbow to spread peanut butter on your bread next time; it does not work as well as your hands. Therefore, it is equally as important to know and understand who we are and what our place is in the body.

When each member knows his or her place and the ministry that they were called to do, they can help the whole-body function more effectively. So how do we discover our place, our ministry, and our gift? How can we work together like we referred to earlier, as a well-oiled machine?

Let us look at the final question first. How can we work together effectively and in harmony with one another? We can look at the human body as an example of how different members or parts fit together. For instance, you would not attach the arm to a hip socket. Nor would the eyes work very well placed in the bottom of one's foot.

Not only is it important to know <u>who</u> you are, it is also important to know what your function is and <u>where</u> you fit into the body. It is therefore vitally important that the five-fold ministry be in place and functioning properly to help the rest of the members find their identity, function, and place. They can therefore fulfill the role for which they were created.

How does the body fit together? We know that our physical body parts come together at certain locations. For instance, our bones come together at joints and those joints are supported by ligaments which reinforce the strength of the joints. They are even further held together by muscles and skin that help protect them from injury.

Encased within this structure are the vital organs that are supported by this bony structure or our skeleton. These are fed and energized via the blood stream which delivers oxygen and food. Where there is no blood, there is no life. The life is in the blood. You get the picture. How does this relate to the body of the church?

Let us look once again at the scripture in Ephesians 4:12: *"For the equipping of the saints for the work of service, to the building up of the body of Christ"*

The word equip in this scripture means to put into place, to set in order, to mend, to prepare …. such as in framing a house or setting a bone in place.

The function of the members of the five-fold ministry which we will study in more depth in the coming chapters is to set the individual bones or members into their proper place. We can also look at the scripture in **Ezekiel thirty-seven** for further evidence.

³ Then He said to me, "Son of man, can these bones live?" And I answered, "Lord GOD, You Yourself know." ⁴ Again He said to me, "Prophesy over these bones and say to them, 'You dry bones, hear the word of the LORD.' ⁵ This is what the Lord GOD says to these bones: 'Behold, I am going to make ˡbreath enter you so that you may come to life. ⁶ And I will attach tendons to you, make flesh grow back on you, cover you with skin, and put breath in you so *that you may come to life; and you will know that I am the LORD.'"*

Ezekiel prophesied to the dead bones, and they came together in their proper place. We were once dead as well, dead in our sin. But as we accepted Jesus as our Savior, that which was dead became alive in Him. We were like those dead bones that came alive once again. He goes on to speak of placing breath back in them. We know that with the newness of life we experience as newborns babes in Christ, we are given the breath of God; his Holy Spirit comes to live within us.

Through the blood of Christ, we are given newness of life. His blood cleanses us and reconnects us to our source, our Heavenly Father. So, we see Ezekiel calling the bones to come together. Just as the bones of our physical body come together so do the bones of the body of Christ, which we are as his members. We are those once dead bones coming together at the joints with new life.

Colossians 2:19 *"and not holding fast to the head, from whom the entire body, being supplied and held together by the joints and ligaments, grows with a growth which is from God."*

Joints in the body of Christ are right relationships with one another so that we might be rightly fit together in the body with one another. The ligaments are the attitudes which we come together with. Good attitudes foster good relationships and strengthen the bond of the body in peace.

Ephesians 4: 1 - 7 see below.

Therefore I, the prisoner of the Lord, implore you to walk in a manner worthy of the calling with which you have been called, 2 with all humility and gentleness, with patience, showing tolerance for one another in love, 3 being diligent to preserve the unity of the Spirit in the bond of peace. 4 There is one body and one Spirit, just as also you were called in one hope of your calling ; 5 one Lord, one faith, one baptism, 6 one God and Father of all who is over all and through all and in all. 7 But to each one of us grace was given according to the measure of Christ's gift.

The bond that holds the whole body together is peace, but it must be done in the attitude of humility, gentleness, patience, and love. As we walk in the Spirit and not in our own flesh, we bear the fruit of the Spirit. Walking in the Spirit and in love creates a bond of peace and unity in the body of Christ.

Verse seven talks about the gift of Christ which we are given in measure. It is our gift of grace, freely given and not earned. Therefore, we are never to give glory to the gift or the bearer but to the gift giver which is God. It says we have received the gift in measure. That is because none of us possess all seven grace gifts in their fullness, for if we did, we would be Christ. He is the only one that possessed all seven of these gifts in the fullness of each of the gifts. We are given a measure of the gift of Christ.

If you can, visualize Christ as seven parts that come together as a whole, like seven pieces of a pie. Each of us in the body has a piece or measure, but when we fit our measure with the other measures of our fellow members in the body, we become a whole. Love is the final bond that holds us all together in unity.

> **Colossians 3:14** "Beyond all these things put on love, which is the perfect bond of unity."

The second question we wanted to address in this chapter was the issue of how can someone discover their gift? What steps can you take to uncover and identify the gifting of God within you?

Seven steps to discover your gift.

Let us begin by looking at the following scripture.

Therefore I urge you, brethren, by the mercies of God, to present your bodies a living and holy sacrifice, acceptable to God, which is your spiritual service of worship. 2 And do not be conformed to this world, but be trans-formed by the renewing of your mind, so that you may prove what the will of God is, that which is good and acceptable and perfect. Romans 12:1-2

The first thing Paul is advising in the passage is that we present our bodies as a living sacrifice. You are probably thinking, wait a moment, I thought sacrifices ended in the Old Testament with the old covenant. What kind of sacrifice do I have to make in the New Testament?

It is true that sacrifices were made for one's sins in the old testament. Jesus did away with the old covenant sacrifice, but as we are admonished to take up our own cross and follow him. Where are we to follow Him? Into the waters of baptism of course, where we sacrifice the old man to put on the new one, the Christ. (Mark 8:34-35)

Step Number One: Give Up the Old You

How does one make their body a living sacrifice? By giving up the old lifestyle and allowing the new lifestyle to become our way of life. In doing so, we choose to deny the unhealthy pleasures of our old sinful life, thus styling our lives after Christ, becoming an imitator of Him.

Step Number Two: Renew your mind and change your behavior.

Repentance begins with a change of heart, but that change must be accompanied by the action of changing one's behavior. As we study the word and are committed to adhering to that which the Holy Spirit shows us, not in word only but also in deed, we will discover that we are being transformed from glory to glory. Our mind is renewed or regenerated through the application of the word of God within our heart, resulting in a change of direction and action.

Step Number Three: Find the Will of God

The will of God should be proven in your life. This is a progressive revelation...from glory to glory. In other words, it is, good, acceptable, and perfect. It must always line up with the word. The will of God will bring a sense of peace and wellbeing...

Step Number Four: Remain Humble

Humility is a decision; it is not an emotion. One must determine in their heart to not think more highly of themselves than they ought to (Romans 12:3). For the same reason, one should not wallow in self-pity or a sense of inferiority.

Giving God the credit for who you are and the gift that he has given will help you remain submitted to glorifying Him. Humility is God's way to success and promotion. Humility is not a sense of inferiority, but a true reflection of who you are in Him.

Step Number Five: Exercise Your Faith

Faith is your spiritual muscle so stretch it out and build it up. What you do not use you will lose. After all, faith without works is dead. So, celebrate, work it out, and try your faith; be a daredevil for Jesus. Just remember not to put God to foolish tests, but always walk in the Spirit and live by faith. Do not allow fear to reign in your life. Just trust in Him. Without faith it is impossible to please God (Hebrews 11:6)!

Step Number Six: Find your place in the body.

Where do you fit in? Through the renewing of your mind and the help of the five-fold ministry you will soon discover not only your identity in Christ, but also your gifts, talents, and ministry.

Step Number Seven: Discover and minister through your gift.

As you begin to grow in his word, your gifts, talents, and areas of service will become self-evident, like the transformation that takes place when the caterpillar emerges from the cocoon as a butterfly. No one can deny what the butterfly has become. Caterpillars cannot fly, butterflies do.

What is the purpose and the benefits of ministering through your motivational gift?

- ➤ Purpose – Your purpose is to fulfill the call of God upon your life and experience wholeness in Him.
- ➤ Benefits – Our personality gifts make us interdependent with one another, eliminating competition, liberating us to fulfill our ministry, and giving us a sense of personal fulfillment.

> Our gifts and mutual submission to one another bring the church into a greater level of maturity

Church growth is not just about numbers, church growth is about maturing the body of Christ. As the individual members of the body find their rightful place, begin to exercise their gifts, and fulfill their ministry, the church will grow.

The goal is to grow up…into the fullness and stature of Jesus Christ. The goal is to expand the Kingdom of God in the earth. Christ is the head, but we are his body, and we are to fulfill his ministry here upon earth.

How do we become Christ's body upon the earth?

When each individual member finds their place, fulfills their ministry using their gifts; the Holy Spirit will begin to flow, and the body will become Christ here upon the earth.

The discovery of personal talents and personality tendencies that hint at our calling may be seen early in life.

Innate tendencies that hint at our inborn purpose may be evidenced even before we begin living for the Lord. For instance…

I remember as a child desiring to take piano lessons, my parents enrolled me in tap dancing lessons instead. After two years of weekly lessons and listening to my complaints, they finally realized that I had two left feet. The ability to dance was not one of my gifts.

The desire of my heart was to play the piano, and so I did. You see where your treasure is, there will your heart be also. The seemingly insignificant dreams and desires can be subtle hints to who you are, even as a child.

As an adult I committed by life to the Lord and my ability to play the piano opened a door of opportunity. I spent many years as the part of praise and worship teams and watched as God matured the gift. Investing my time and talent to bring glory to the Lord multiplied the talent I had discovered as a child.

That burning desire I sensed on the inside to play piano was God leading me down the path that he had chosen. He does not need to speak in an audible voice or from a burning bush to reveal himself to you. Sometimes, in fact most times, it is simply that still small voice you hear within saying here is the way, walk in the path that I have chosen for you.

When we listen to that voice and hear what he says, it will usually seem bigger than life. If what he is telling you is bigger than you can imagine for yourself, that is an excellent indicator that the thought came directly from God. Assess it, try it, and prove it… if it is God's word, it will come to pass in your life.

Be willing to step out of the boat and walk by faith where the unction leads. When you heed the voice and follow His lead you can be assured that it will take you somewhere great!

Chapter Seven:

Gifts of the Son

What is the purpose of the Five-fold ministry?

The five-fold ministry is the gift of the Son to the church. The purpose of the five-fold ministry is to lead and guide the saints from spiritual infancy to spiritual maturity. Helping them to find and fulfill the will of God for their life. How?

1. Help them discover who they are and what their purpose is in Christ.
2. Help them identify their gifts and gifting and how to utilize them.
3. Help them to find their place in the body.
4. Help them to develop their own personal ministry.

1 Corinthians 12:4-6 *"Now there are varieties of gifts, but the same Spirit. 5 **And there are varieties of ministries, and the same Lord.** 6 There are varieties of effects, but the same God who works all things in all persons."*

Once again, we want to focus on the scripture in verse five. There are varieties of ministries, and the same Lord, in the King James Version it refers to them as <u>administrations</u>. In the very beginning of this book, we talked about how a ketchup factory created ketchup from the raw product of tomatoes. We identified three primary departments that are necessary to complete this process and one of those was the administrative department.

The administrative department is responsible for the coordination of all departments and operations. Without this department the bills would not be paid, the supplies would not get ordered, and people would not get hired to work as the employees for the company.

> Ephesians 4:11 "And He gave some as apostles, and some as prophets, and some as evangelists, and some as pastors and teachers, 12 for the equipping of the saints for the work of service, to the building up of the body of Christ; 13 until we all attain to the unity of the faith, and of the knowledge of the Son of God, to a mature man, to the measure of the stature which belongs to the fullness of Christ.
>
> 14 As a result, we are no longer to be children, tossed here and there by waves and carried about by every wind of doctrine, by the trickery of men, by craftiness in deceitful scheming; 15 but speaking the truth in love, we are to grow up in all aspects into Him who is the head, even Christ, 16 from whom the whole body, being fitted and held together by what every joint supplies, according to the proper working of each individual part, causes the growth of the body for the building up of itself in love."

Five-Fold Ministry Gifts

The administrative gifts within the body are the gifts of Christ to the church that we know as the five-fold ministry. The word "ministries" above in the original Greek is the word "diakonia" and it means, to command, or to execute the commands of others.

Earlier we discussed a straightforward way to remember the five different offices within the five-fold ministry. Think of them as the individual fingers on your hand. If one of your fingers was missing, it would decrease your ability to use that hand. It is equally important that the five offices of the five-fold ministry be in their proper places and working effectively enabling the church to mature and grow appropriately as it was meant to do.

The Apostle

The Apostle in the Greek is Apostolos meaning one that is sent; much like our modern-day ambassadors. They were commissioned with a message and empowered with supernatural powers.

They cannot be appointed by man and the office cannot be earned through service, study, acts or honorable deeds. Unlike the other offices, the Apostle is often able to perform any of the other four functions in the five-fold ministry. They often coordinate the five-fold ministry team and the work that they do to advance the kingdom.

The apostle establishes new kingdom ministries, preparing the foundation work and raising up local leadership. The apostle then encourages and strengthens those he oversees. He is also called to bring discipline when it is required. For instance, in just one example the Apostle Paul wrote to the Corinthians regarding a matter of immorality of one in their own body. (1 Corinthians 5) Those who have great authority, will also have great responsibility for those they lead.

> *"…From everyone who has been given much, much will be demanded; and to whom they entrusted much, of him they will ask all the more."* (Luke 12:48b)

The apostle may evangelize, pastor, prophesy, teach, and the office is confirmed by signs and wonders. While some may claim that the office of apostle was meant only for the original twelve disciples, the biblical text extends this classification to others as well.

Let us take another look at the work of the Apostle Paul. Who could deny his calling and ability to function in the office of apostle? He was not one of the original twelve, but he wrote more of our bible than any other single human being. He experienced beatings and torture but is credited with taking the good news to the Gentile believers despite the harsh reality of persecutions he was forced to endure. He preached the word, taught, and performed signs, wonders, and miracles; even to the point of raising the dead.

Paul planted churches and established leadership. (1 Corinthians 3:10) Paul is probably one of the most noteworthy of the apostles not to diminish the work of his peers, both from the past and the present. He even held Peter responsible for his hypocritical behavior when he separated himself from the Gentiles and would only eat with the Jews (Galatians 2:11).

Do we still need apostles to take responsibility for planting new churches, working with the other four offices, raising up leadership in the church today? Of course, we do! We will continue to need those called of God to function in the capacity of apostle until the day Jesus returns to take his bride.

The first twelve apostles were not the only apostles, they were simply the first. We have just emerged from a period of history where many dismissed the significance of the Prophet and Apostle in the modern-day church. Fortunately, the tide is turning. The acceptance of Apostles is increasing. They are again being recognized as valuable and necessary assets to the body of Christ.

The Prophet

Like the apostle, the term prophet is frequently associated with the prophets of old. Prophets like Samuel, Ezekiel, and Jeremiah who spoke the truth even when it was not convenient to do so.

In an era of seeker friendly, don't rock the boat mentalities, some seem to think we no longer need prophets in the body of Christ. One could argue that it is this thought process that has potentially led to a weakened lukewarm church. Churches where the move of Holy Spirit is discouraged in the interest of not offending those who may not understand.

Nothing could be further from the truth. Now more than ever before, we need the insight and revelation of prophets. They can provide valuable guidance and direction to the modern-day church. Rather than discouraging the exercising of gifts and ministries we need to encourage it! All members of the five-fold ministry, including the prophet, are needed for the equipping of the church.

The prophet is the second in our list of five-fold ministry offices and is responsible for speaking the heart of God and foretelling future events. God does nothing except he tells his prophets first (Amos 3:7). The prophet is a teacher with a consistent manifestation of the revelation gifts plus prophecy.

Although we are urged in the scriptures to covet to prophesy, the gift of prophesy alone does not make one a prophet. The scriptures also tell us that all may prophesy, but we know not all are called to hold the office of a prophet.

Those who stand in the office of a prophet are once again those who are called and set apart for the office by Jesus. Unlike the gift of prophesy, they may be used to correct and admonish the body when needed. The prophet was and is a visionary called of God to function as a watchman and is responsible for speaking forth both God's will and His intentions.

We have biblical examples of both men and women who stood in the office of a prophet. It does not matter if they are a man or woman, Greek or Jew; they must simply be called, chosen, and set aside to fulfill the office by God. The evidence will become obvious as the fruit falls from the lips of those who speak. We can see in the word of God prophets who changed their environment both in the supernatural and the natural, as God led them.

Prophets receive their message from God in a variety of diverse ways including visions, dreams, declarations, or through a knowing from within (the still small "voice," 1 Kings 19). The prophet may speak the word of the Lord, write it, or demonstrate it through the way they live their life. A perfect example of this was Hosea whose life was a living parable. God instructed him to marry a prostitute in Hosea 1-3. This was a dramatic demonstration of God's relationship to Israel.

Other terms that may be used for prophet are seers or oracles of God, they define the nature of their ministry to the body. Although proof of one's calling in this area will be confirmed by a fulfillment of their words. We must take care to remember that some prophesy is conditional based upon the hearer's response. Take for example the warning of Jonah the reluctant prophet, the warning he spoke was heeded and the people were spared.

Prophets are not always welcomed with open arms because of the corrective nature of some prophesy. The true test of a prophet is that they are willing to suffer hardship to fulfill their calling and to deliver the word of the Lord to his people.

The Evangelist

The five-fold ministry office of the evangelist is filled by one called of God and who proclaims the good news to those who are outside of the kingdom of God, with a focus of bringing men and women to Christ. They may preach or teach the word.

They should be well established in the word and filled with the Holy Ghost. The work that they do may include the working of signs, wonders, miracles, as well as deliverance. Their calling will be evidenced by the souls won through their ministry. They will lead new converts into baptism and direct them into a local body or start one if necessary.

They are not called to minister to one specific body of believers. The evangelist is usually one who travels to win the lost and is the one who breaks the ground for the work of the other ministries. He is the forerunner.

****** In this 2022 update I realized that there is much more to be said about this marvelous gift of God to the body of Christ. Evangelists like George Whitfield, Kathryn Kulman, Smith Wigglesworth, Billy Graham, William Seymour, Oral Roberts have all left a lasting impression on the previous generations. Some of you may even remember the tent crusades of the R. W. Schambach, T.L. Osborne, and A. A. Allen, Aimee Semple McPherson… or at least you have heard of them.

Some of you may be aware that a new surge of evangelism is making its way throughout the nation not the least of which started in a tent in California with Mario Murillo. Once again thousands are reportedly being saved, delivered, and healed across our nation. Many believe that a great new awakening is already in process with an incoming harvest of souls that some project could number in the billions. Not only is the office of evangelist needed, but it is vital in the times we are currently experiencing. Many suggest that this is the great end time harvest that we have been anticipating prior to the return of Jesus Christ.

The Pastor

The Greek word for pastor is poiman meaning shepherd. We typically think of the shepherd carrying the rod and staff to lead, guide, and direct or correct the sheep. Here the pastor is the shepherd of God's sheep. Called to tend, teach, protect, correct, and feed them.

Those called to pastor the flock should do so with a sincere heart for those they are called to lead. They willingly lay down their own personal needs to care for those they are called to minister to, they serve sacrificially. They will care for the flock in many different capacities including but not limited to, visitation, prayer, preaching, teaching, ministering to the sick and the widows, and watching out for those who might want to do harm to the flock.

Their responsibilities may be diverse but primarily they must be given to study and prayer, leading by example through a spirit filled life. They are to lead and guide, not drive the sheep. They are not to dictate or take advantage of the flock but to lay down their own personal agendas for the needs of those to which they provide oversight. They must be committed and loyal to those they lead humbling themselves to become a servant even as Jesus did by example.

Although they are responsible for the care of the sheep, they must also take care not to neglect their own personal growth and relationship to the Lord. The pastor's first responsibility is to the Lord, not to the sheep. The true pastor exalts the Lord Jesus Christ and not themselves. Many of these attributes mentioned in this section may also be applicable to anyone who is called as an elder in the local church.

The Teacher

The fifth and final gift we want to explore is the gift of the teacher. The teacher expounds, exhorts, explains, and teaches the word of the Lord to believers, to strengthen their faith and understanding of the gospel. They teach doctrine, ethics, reverence, history, and the timeline for events that are found within the pages of our bible.

The teacher helps to mature the body by teaching the basic beliefs and doctrines laid out in our scripture and explaining how to apply those principals to one's life. They take even the most intricate and deep precepts and make them accessible to those they teach. They have a knack for taking what seems difficult to comprehend and opening it up for all to understand. While the teacher is especially gifted in the ability to explain biblical truths, all elders should be willing to teach both in word and deed.

I once heard a prophetic word given to a believer called to minister through the gift of teaching. The word stated, "you will take concepts that are difficult to grasp and present them in such a way that even the young can understand. It is like taking cookies from the top shelf of a bakery cart and placing them on the bottom so that all can partake." Well folks, that is exactly what a teacher does. They uncover revelations of the word and help believers comprehend how to apply them successfully to their personal lives.

Closing Thoughts on the Five-fold Ministry

Christ came to build a body of related believers. He wants to set the bones of the body in place. Let us once again revisit the scripture in Ezekiel 37: 1-10. Ezekiel was told to prophesy to the dead bones. He was to call them to come together. If the bones are not placed in the right position in the body, the proper function of that bone will not be realized.

Let us reflect on this point for a moment. Members of the body are called to come together as one. Coming together requires more than occupying the same space. We must come together in thought, deed, and purpose as well. We are to become a team, a well coordinated army with a common divine assignment to establish the Kingdom. This may require personal sacrifice to accomplish the goal for the common good.

Where Do You Fit?

Just as bones in the human body have a set place where they belong, so do the members of the body (the bones in our scripture). If the bones are not placed in the proper location, they cannot effectively fulfill their purpose. For instance, those called to teach may not be as effective in an administrative role of the church such as an accountant. That is not to say an accountant cannot teach. We must recognize the gift and place the person in their proper place for their specific gift and calling to develop and flow.

Gifts may not be obvious at first, especially in new believers. As the new believer begins to grow, mature, and exercise their faith, their gifts should become self-evident. It is the role of those in leadership, especially those in the offices of the five-fold ministry, to help each one discover their gift, develop it, and find their own specific place within the body. It is as each individual member finds their place and fulfills it that the whole body can mature and grow as the church.

I have witnessed in my own ministry how those who are called to a specific ministry will tend to be drawn to others who are already functioning in that role. Those who have a yearning to preach the word will watch those around them that are already doing what they feel called to do. They will then seek that person out to learn all that they can, utilizing them as a mentor.

Those in leadership are wise to learn all they can about each gift in the body of Christ so that they can identify the gifts in operation. It is equally important to spot any gifts that are currently lying dormant. Once they do so, they can then help to nurture that gift through teaching and mentoring. Placing that person in safe settings where they can begin to exercise their gifts will help them develop their gifting.

Those who are called to preach may not want to start out in front of a congregation of 500. Sometimes a small cell group or nursing home ministry will give them the experience they need to develop the gift in greater proportion. Once their gift matures, their confidence and skill develops... then perhaps they can tackle larger preaching assignments.

So, what is the responsibility of the five-fold ministry within the scope of maturing the church and preparing the bride of Christ for her wedding day?

I want to refer you back to the scripture in Ephesians 4 verse 12 "for the equipping of the saints for the work of service, to the building up of the body of Christ;" It is the purpose of the five-fold ministry to equip the body. Christ came to build a body of believers and his gift to accomplish that was the five-fold ministry gifts.

As those five offices are filled and functioning, they will lead the unsaved, bring them into the salvation experience and equip them to become a mature body. The word equip, in conversational Greek, means to outfit an army. Are we not the army of the Lord?

Formed, Equipped, and Outfitted

In Ephesians 1:22 we see the body is formed with Christ as the Head, and in chapter four it is equipped. In chapter six however it is taken one step further, the body is outfitted as an army. Do you see the progression? The church goes from equipped body to victorious army, but not just any army… they are the glorious, victorious army of the Lord. Praise the Lord… but the best is yet to come.

The goal of the body is to grow up into the fullness of Christ. This can only be accomplished when all the individual members come together fulfilling their portion of the ministry of the body. The body cannot reach full maturity and attain perfection in Him unless it is in the bond of peace and in the strength of His love.

Practical Application

Over the past almost forty years in ministry, I have had the honor and privilege of helping many who like me, were trying to find their place in the body. Those who were like minded and gifted in a similar fashion would naturally seek me out and ask my advice.

Many simply needed encouragement to help them develop the confidence to step out and start using their gifts. That is why it is so vitally important for those in leadership to have an abundant grasp and working knowledge of all the gifts and roles in the body. How else can these new believers' roles and gifts be recognized?

Based upon this knowledge, we can begin to identify those called to teach, preach, and lead; helping to nurture them in the areas that they are gifted. This is the role of leadership, to develop the sheep and lead them into maturity to take their place in service, using whatever their gift or role may be. Every believer has a place, and it is important that we help them find it for the profit of the whole body.

I have found it beneficial to set up safe scenarios in which these less mature believers have an opportunity to discover their gifts and talents. For instance, watch for people with an undeveloped gift and then create opportunities for them to begin learning how to use that gift. Start from wherever they are and help direct them to where they are going.

In my role as a teacher, I would invite others to share with me in the teaching responsibilities, giving them small portions to do in the lessons until they felt confident enough to do more. As they progressed, more and more responsibility would be given to them.

In preaching, I had many come to me with a yearning to preach. They came and asked how I got started. I assured them that I did very poorly when I first started out; the important thing is <u>not</u> how good you are the first time. The important thing is that there is a first time, and a second time, and so on until the gift develops.

You see, there is a progression, for as you use your gift it begins to develop and grow. (You must have that gift to begin with of course.) Think back to the parable of the talents and the pounds. We are to be wise stewards of the gift God placed within us, and he will bring the increase. Don't worry about how good you are, just use what you've got, and you will see increase and growth! Those that are faithful in the little things will be entrusted with more. (Matthew 25:21)

Of course, this works in reverse as well. If someone thinks they have a gift but does not, just give them little opportunities to prove themselves, in a safe setting. This will help them prove their gift or recognize that they lack. A true gift or ministry will always bear fruit if it is truly from God, and if that person is being faithfully submitted to the Lord.

As others came to me for assistance, I sought an opportunity for them to begin using their preaching skills. With the senior pastor's blessing, I found a nursing home that needed people to hold services on a weekly basis. I was able to secure opportunities for our young preachers to develop and polish their preaching skills.

I did not just leave them out there on their own, however. I went with them especially in the beginning, or I would counsel them on how to get started. Then I would follow their progress and supported them as they took the first brave steps, fulfilling their purpose. It can be scary at first if you have never spoken in public; that is why we are not alone. As the five-fold ministry takes its place and fulfills its role, the whole body will begin to grow and develop.

Growth of the Church

Much has been said in recent years on the growth of one's church. In the day of mega churches, the focus can become more about the numbers and prestige than getting people saved and discipled.

This can potentially lead to a willingness to compromise our basic judeo Christian principles; the ones we hold dear, all for the sake of growing a larger church. It is a slippery slope that we do not want to engage. We must guard our hearts and check our own motives to avoid falling into this trap. We must always use caution when approaching this subject and so we will.

While we want to reach more people for Christ, we must continue to be accountable for our motive. So, let us address the question of numerical growth first. When I say this, I mean it in the terms of seeing more people born again and discipled. Keeping all this in mind, let us discuss reaching more with the gospel message. Reaching more via addition can be a slow and sometimes laborious task. See in the diagram below.

Reaching More: The Addition Model

1st three months 4 people x 2 = 8 new disciples

2nd three months 4 people x 2 + 8 more new disciples

3rd three months 4 people x 2 = 8 more

4th three months 4 people x 2 = 8 more

By adding, the church grew by 32 new converts in one year.

If you go to the book of Acts, you can see that after the body of believers were filled with the Holy Ghost which was power from on high, they immediately went out and begin to share the good news with others. At first the church experienced growth through the process of addition; in Acts 2 they began adding to the church daily.

> **⁴⁷** *Praising God, and having favour with all the people. And the Lord added to the church daily such as should be saved*

As we continue to read, we find the dynamics have changed in the 6th chapter of Acts verse 1.

> *"And in those days, when the number of the disciples was multiplied"*

I do not think the author made a mistake here. Once disciples began making disciples, they in turn did the same. They wanted to share their good fortune with others and the good news spread like wildfire! Disciples, discipling others, who in turn discipled even more new believers. This is it no longer adding to the church daily, but it becomes a multiplication of new believers.

You know yourself that if you want something to grow, multiplication is much better than addition. If someone wanted to increase my income, I would want them to multiply it, not just add to it.

> ## Church Growth by Multiplication
>
> 1st three months 4 people x 2 = <u>8 new</u> disciples
>
> 2nd three months original 4 + 8 new people =
>
> 12 people x 2 = <u>24 new</u> disciples
>
> 3rd three months the 12 plus their 24 new converts =
>
>   36 x 2 = <u>72 new people</u>
>
> 4th three months 36 + 72 new ones x 2=
>
> 216 new disciples in just one year just because 4 people in a church were determined to fulfill the great commission of Christ.

How does church growth go from the principals of addition to those of multiplication? Simple, you take new believers and mature them, teaching them how to evangelize. Then you send them out to do the same; making new converts and raising up others to go out and win new souls. See in the first box how just four people can cause the church to grow.

Now if those same four people teach the new disciples how to lead others to Christ as well, and add their results to the mix, look at what happens to the numbers.

Just 4 people in a congregation dedicated to discipling by multiplication can increase the church by 216 new members in one year. I don't know about you, but I like 216 a lot better than 32.

Do you see why it is so important that we not just get them saved? Who goes through the process of bringing a new baby into the world only to abandon them in the delivery room? As Christians, we need to take responsibility to do more than just get them saved. We need to mentor and disciple them until they are of full age.

Then they can take their rightful place in the body so that we can take the Kingdom of God to the entire world. Five-fold ministry, it is time to arise and take your place so that we can fulfill the great commission of Christ.

A Better Measure of Growth

Remember, growth is not about growing a bigger church but about reaching more for Christ. It is about seeing the body of believers arise and take their place as the ecclesia of God. It is about governing here on earth and establishing the kingdom. Amen.

Chapter Eight:

The Gifts of Manifestation

Word of Wisdom	Working of Miracles
Word of Knowledge	Gifts of healing
Discerning of spirits	Faith
Prophecy	Tongues
Interpretation of Tongues	

The manifestation gifts are *varieties* of gifts given to us by the Holy Spirit and can be imparted by the laying on of hands. They are, as the name implies, a manifestation of the Spirit. It is interesting to note that the number nine is the number of divine perfection.

Some also refer to these gifts as the sign gifts perhaps because they are a demonstration or sign to all that witness them in operation. The nine spiritual gifts are given to empower us for the work of the ministry. They are frequently divided into three groups of three. There are three gifts of revelation, three gifts of power, and three gifts of inspiration or utterance.

> Now there are varieties of gifts, but the same Spirit.
> 1 Corinthians 12:4

The bible is full of the supernatural acts and works of God. It is impossible to read the New Testament and not notice incident after incident of the miraculous, first through the hands of Jesus in the gospels. Even after his ascension, the acts continued to be performed by his disciples.

Paul, during his long ministry in Ephesus, had many signs and wonders follow his ministry. In Acts 19:11 we see an account where "special miracles" were accomplished through the hands of Paul. The word "special" in this case meaning they were not the ordinary types of miracles, not that any miracles are normal. These specific miracles were more miraculous than the signs that had been witnessed prior to this incident.

As we search for reasons these miraculous incidents took place, we can see that it had a divine connection to the preaching of the gospel. First, it was a sign to attract people to hear the gospel, and secondly to authenticate the ministry. This is how we get the term "sign gifts."

An investigation of the Christian people of the New Testament reveals that the people of that era were not so different from us. They knew sorrow and joy, riches and poverty, strength and weakness, health, and sickness and yet everywhere they went the supernatural power and miraculous were manifested.

What exactly did they do in their meetings and churches? Praying (Acts 6:5-6), preaching (Acts 8:12), singing of hymns and spiritual songs, and psalms, (Colossians 3:16), the Lord's Supper (Matt.26:26-30), collections (1 Corinthians 16:1-2), fasting (Acts 13:2). Their meeting was not much different from ours; they were open to Holy Spirit and experienced the supernatural manifestation of his presence.

These people had intensely vivid experiences with the Holy Spirit, and they knew when, where, and how he came. This is evidenced by Paul when he asked them in Acts 19:2 if they had experienced him since they believed. Yes, the Holy Spirit is not an it, he is a person and a member of the Godhead.

Those who were baptized in the Spirit spoke in tongues and prophesied. This shows an obvious connection between the baptism of the Spirit and the gifts of the Spirit. The word manifestation in the Greek (phanerosis) means a shining forth or revealing. The Holy Spirit reveals God shining through us as we exercise his gifts.

The supernatural should be an everyday experience to us. This includes the operation of the gifts. Just expect it to happen. They <u>should</u> happen as we are partakers of the divine nature with Christ.

When earnestly studying the gifts of manifestation there are three chapters in 1 Corinthians that are the most notable on the subject, they are chapters 12, 13, and 14. Chapter 12 lists the gifts and the different administrations but mentions that it is the same Spirit; it is the power chapter. Chapter 14 is the love chapter and how to use the gifts in love. This is an important aspect to keep in mind. We need to operate in love.

Chapter 13 is the integral link between the two chapters explaining what the gifts are like when they <u>are not</u> used in love compared to how they are when they <u>are</u> used in love. These three chapters tie in perfectly with the scripture found in 2 Timothy 1:7 which tells us that "We have not received the spirit of fear but of power, and of love, and of a sound mind."

The words "is given" in 1 Corinthians 12:7 is the word "Didotai" in the Greek, which is in a present continual tense.

> *"But to each one is given the manifestation of the Spirit for the common good."*

This simply means that it is not given one time only, but it is continually being given. It is not about our ability but about our availability. Therefore, none of us needs to fear that we cannot or will not be used by God, for Holy Spirit gives us the gifts, *severally as he wills*, that empower us to minister to the body.

God is the God of Order

We all have a gift from Holy Spirit to contribute. We must always keep in mind that the gifts are to be used properly and in order.

> *"for God is not a God of confusion, but of peace. As in all the churches of the saints."* 1 Corinthians 14:33

Order is to be maintained within the service as the Lord is not the author of confusion. Therefore, we must be mindful of the protocol to be utilized in accordance with our scriptures and in accordance with the governing offices of the local body. The one who bears the gift controls when, where, and how they exercise the gift but it is always to be under the leading of the Holy Spirit. The Holy Spirit is a gentleman.

Let us begin with the three Gifts of Revelation which give us the ability to know.

Word of Wisdom

The word of wisdom is the supernatural revelation of divine purpose. It is not wisdom in and of itself, but it is a word of wisdom. This implies that it is not complete within itself but merely a portion or measure which we receive. God is all knowing so whatever portion he chooses to reveal to his servant, it is only a part of the fullness of the wisdom of God.

C. Peter Wagner referred to this gift as the ability to know the mind of the Holy Spirit in such a way as to know how to apply that knowledge to meet the needs of the body of Christ. It is a foretelling of the future and is one of the greatest of the revelatory gifts. It is not to be confused with the gift of prophesy which is not foretelling in nature. Prophets are also known as seers, and they speak of the future because of the gift of the word of wisdom.

People with this gift have a divine insight and a keen perception that make them natural problem solvers. They are very sensitive to the needs and feelings of others and can navigate through a difficulty to bring resolution. This gift makes them excellent consultants.

Word of Knowledge

The word of knowledge is a supernatural revelation of facts, a discovery of truth that could only have been revealed by the disclosure of Holy Spirit. For instance, when Jesus spoke to the woman at the well, he spoke to her of facts he could not have known except they were revealed to him by the divine mind of God.

This gift is often confused with the gift of the Word of Wisdom, but as we explained earlier the word of Wisdom is the ability to know how to apply that truth to life. I can tell you of one instance where the Lord used me to minister to a woman who had been making statements contrary to the Lord's word for her life. I had never heard her make these statements, but I heard the statements repeatedly in my mind like a broken record.

Finally, I approached her and asked if I could pray with her. She was quite receptive, so I began to pray, and I found myself repeating those same words directly to her with a message that she was not to say them anymore. The thoughts she was rehearsing in her mind and expressing to others were contrary to the will of God.

There was then a divine explanation through the exercising of the word of wisdom explaining to her why what she had said was not true. The woman was quite amazed as she knew that I could not have heard the conversation that I repeated to her. She realized that the message had to be divinely inspired as I could have had no knowledge of the situation on my own. Her husband was present as I prayed and confirmed that she had been repeating these things.

God truly touched this lady through an exercising of the gift of the Word of Knowledge. I trust that she continued to walk in her true identity in Christ and no longer listened to the lies of the enemy. "The thief comes to steal, kill, and destroy..." and that applies to our identity, but Jesus came that we might have life, and that in abundance. (See John 10:10) God cares when the enemy tries to beat us down with lies about who we are, he cares enough to expose the truth.

> *"Therefore, there is now no condemnation at all for those who are in Christ Jesus."* Romans 8:1

Let us review one last time, the revelation of a truth is the Word of Knowledge and the ability to know how to apply that truth to life is the Word of Wisdom. Time to move on now to one last revelatory gift.

Discerning of Spirits

This is a supernatural revelation into the realm of the spirit to know which spirit is in operation whether it is good spirit or an evil spirit. A good example can be found in Acts 13: 9-10 when Paul spoke to Elymas the sorcerer.

It is important to note, this is the gift of Discerning of Spirits, not to be confused with what some refer to as the gift of discernment.

The revelatory gift, Discerning of Spirits, is a gift of truth revealed by the Holy Spirit, it is specific to the distinguishing between spirits, both good and evil. Peter was exercising this gift when he discerned the spirit operating in the story of Ananias and Sapphira. This revelatory gift can be imparted to anyone Holy Spirit choses. It is not learned; it is given as a gift.

On the other hand, Paul in the book of Hebrews talks to us about those who have learned discernment. This is an ability of those who are mature in the Lord to learn the difference between good and bad. They have exercised their spiritual acuity so that they have learned how to distinguish between good and evil. This is a learned ability not a spiritually endowed gift.

> *But solid food is for the mature, who because of practice have their senses trained to distinguish between good and evil.* Hebrews 5:14

In conclusion, just remember that the manifestation gift of Discerning of Spirits cannot be learned or earned. It is a divinely revealed gift of truth, freely given by Holy Spirit that exposes the true spirit in operation. It is a valuable gift made available to the body of Christ. The ability of those who have grown in their relationship with the Lord, walked out and exercised their faith, and through use have learned to discern both good and evil, is also important and to be desired and pursued.

That will complete our discourse of the gifts of revelation. The second set of the three spiritual gifts of manifestation are the gifts of power.

3 Gifts of Power

Faith

This is the supernatural belief in the power of God for the impossible to happen. This is not to be confused with the measure of faith that we each receive. (Romans 12:3) No, the gift of faith is related to the ability to believe God for supernatural happenings.

It is not the same kind of faith we need to believe for salvation. It is not the faith we need to believe God to fulfill his word. This is a far greater gift as it moves the bearer into the realm of believing for the unbelievable and the ability to rest in that knowledge of supernatural provision, protection, and healing.

Supernatural Provision

I heard about a lady who had lost her job and her unemployment had been held up. She was given a ticket to visit relatives over the Christmas vacation, so she went, even though she had no viable income to support her for the trip.

While away, she received another invitation to an important conference. She still had no income, no sign of income in the near future, and bills mounting higher and higher. It seemed ridiculous to take the invitation seriously. In fact, an acquaintance hearing of the invitation, scolded her for even thinking about it at all. Nevertheless, she could not shake the feeling that she was to go.

So, she simply laid it out before the Lord and said, "Lord, if you want me to go you will have to provide the funds." Once again, the situation from all angles was simply impossible, yet she found herself believing that God would make a way for her.

Within three days, three weeks' worth of unemployment was deposited into her account. Then a check arrived, it was more than enough to cover the trip. Finally, she got a phone call from an employer who wanted to start her on orientation for a job that was to only be for one day a week. It hardly seemed worth the trouble, but she went anyway. When she got there, they told her that she was to work full time for 3 -4 weeks to fulfill her orientation.

Within four weeks, she had several thousand dollars in the bank and another $3000 that would arrive before she was to leave to take the trip. Her bills were paid, her trip was paid. She had more than enough to pay for everything she needed to go, and still have money left over.

Do you know what put the icing on the cake? When she got to the location of the meeting and went to rent her car, the agent at the desk took one look at her license and said, "Today is your birthday?" She said yes. Then the agent said to her, "Do you mind if I give you a free upgrade?" Then she pointed to the car sitting outside on the curb, it was a Sebring convertible. The lady drove away in the car in total disbelief. She phoned her friend and said, "You are not going to believe what just happened to now!" You see, that is the kind of God we serve. He is a "more than enough" kind of God.

The Working of Miracles

This is the supernatural intervention and power of God in the course of nature. The first example that comes to mind is the parting of the Red Sea. That was nothing short of a miracle. Of course, there are many others, but that one stands out to me first and foremost. There are some who would argue that God did miracles in bible days, but not in the present days.

Once again, I know of a lady who was driving home from work one night. She was working as a nurse in a nursing home on the second shift. One of the patients had become extremely confused during the evening and had begged her to stay. The nurse knew he was prone to spells of confusion, so she thought nothing of it.

She got into her car to drive the thirty miles to home and turned on the radio. About halfway home she was on top of a hill and descending the other side when the radio began to fade, so she reached over to adjust the station. As she did, the car was suddenly propelled forward at a rapid rate of speed and began to spin about in the opposite direction.

She did not understand what was happening at first but found the car rolling in midair as the other car, the car that had hit her from behind, was pulling away. She was not wearing a seatbelt, so the impact threw her about violently inside the car. She broke the mirror with her forehead; bent the steering wheel with her chest, and her knee broke the knob off the stick shift.

As the car finally landed, by the grace of God on all four wheels, she found herself surrounded by corn on all four sides. The only thing she said as she rolled high above the corn was to cry out to God for help. There was little time for anything else. Now she had somehow survived the crash and the violent ascent and descent from midair into a field of corn. She was so deep into the field, (the full-grown corn surrounding her was still standing) that she had no idea which direction the road might be.

She found herself asking the Lord for help once more. You see the crash had thrown her so high in the air that the corn around her had not been touched. The doors were jammed shut from the crash, and the windows were all cracked, and only the driver's side window was broken out enough for her to attempt to climb out and that had sharp jagged points protruding from the edge.

Fearing the crash and the field of corn may cause the car to suddenly burst into flames, she determined she must get out of the car at any cost, even if she became severely cut from the glass. She asked the Lord for help and pulled her legs up into the seat.

She had no idea how she was going to pull herself out of the window without getting hurt, the jagged points of glass would no doubt slice her up, but she did not care. She just wanted out. So, as she poked her head out of the top portion of the window trying to determine how to get her feet up on the seat. Suddenly she found herself some 35 feet away from the car and outside of the field trying to catch her balance in the ditch.

How did she get there? Even she does not know. One moment she was climbing out the window and the next she was standing alongside the road. She knew that she never finished climbing through the window; nor did she decide on which way to go to reach the road. She was as baffled as everyone else as to how it was possible. How is it that she found herself outside the field on the edge of the road? She knows she did not walk there on her own.

The best part came when another driver who had observed the crash returned to the scene to say, "I thought you had to be dead, so I chased the car that hit you! The person in the car pulled away from me at a speed in excess of 120 mph." The doctors and nurses that treated her at the hospital were all amazed. They told her that she should have been dead, or at least critically hurt. Yet there was not one broken bone, and no cuts deep enough to stitch. They did not even attempt to take x-rays. They did not know what to x-ray!

The doctors, the nurses, and the state highway patrol were left to scratch their heads and wonder at how such a miracle could have happened. I know how, it was an act of God. Miracles still happen, even today. They happen to ordinary people like you and like me. God is a good God.

Gifts of Healing

This is the supernatural ability of God to heal diseases. You will notice that this gift is plural; it is the gifts of healing not the gift of healing. How many gifts are there? I am not certain anyone knows. We know there are many kinds of sickness, and the Lord is capable and willing to heal them all.

Our final category in the realm of the gifts of manifestation, are the three Gifts of Inspiration. They give the bearers the ability to speak.

3 Gifts of Inspiration

Prophesy

This is a supernatural inspiration to give a message in a known tongue. The gift of prophesy is for edification, exhortation, and comfort. To edify means to build up and the word encourages the church. To exhort simply means to encourage one another. It is not foretelling of the future. The bible tells us that we are to covet to prophesy. It also tells us that all may prophesy (1 Corinthians 14:31). Why? Because by doing so we build, encourage, and comfort one another.

An example of a prophesy might be the following:

> *"The Lord says, 'I love you with an everlasting love. I will never leave you nor forsake you. I see what you are going through. Do*

not fear for I am God, and I am right beside you and will hold your hand. Nothing can harm you for you are my child and I take care of all that are mine. If I know the number of hairs on your head, then I certainly know what it is you are facing, and you need not be afraid for I am with you always. The Lord is a good God, and he gives good gifts to His children. You are blessed with my favor but more importantly you have my love.'"

This is the gift that Phillip's four daughters had, they could exhort and comfort. They could not foretell the future because they were not called to the office of a prophet (1 Corinthians 14:3). John Eckhardt in his book, "God Still Speaks" said this, "We encourage believers who are not called into the office of a prophet to stay within the limits of edification, exhortation, and comfort. Prophets are the ones who have the authority to speak beyond the limit of edification, exhortation, and comfort."[4]

This gift is subject to the one using it, that means they can control it and must know when, where, and how to do so. One must know how to prophesy in accordance with the regulations and order set forth in the body of believers they are in. In 1 Corinthians 14:29 it tells us to let two or three speak and let the others judge.

Some churches ask that a word be shared with a leader first to gain permission to release it to the congregation. It is important to know the rules in the church where you are so that you may use your gift decently and in order. Once again, God is not the author of confusion. Knowing when, where, and how to release a word of prophesy comes with experience.

---

[4] "God Still Speaks" John Eckhardt, published by Charisma House.

Diverse Kinds of Tongues

This is the supernatural ability to speak in an unknown tongue. It is not to be confused with one's prayer language. We know that on the day of Pentecost the Holy Spirit was given and they began to speak in tongues. They were not exercising the sign gift of tongues on this specific occasion. They were speaking with their new prayer language.

The sign gift is the divine ability to give a message in tongues that will then require an interpretation. If one gives a message in tongues and there is no one there to interpret it, then the one giving the message should provide the interpretation as well.

Interpretation of Tongues

This is the divine supernatural ability to give the interpretation of a message in tongues. Holy Spirit reveals the meaning to the bearer of this gift. It is not a word for word translation, but rather an interpretation of the message being said. This is like the interpretation of a speaker in a foreign land. The interpreter does not translate word for word, but the content of the message is repackaged in the phrases common to the listeners making it easy to understand.

Conclusion

All these gifts are supernatural and require faith to bring them into operation.

Chapter Nine:

Motivational Gifts

I tried out for the senior class play in high school. I had played the main part in the one-act play competition two years running so I had my heart set on one of the main characters in this play. Besides, I had less competition for this play because only people in the senior class could audition.

They began the tryouts with the smaller parts first. Not wanting to put all my eggs in one basket, I decided it would be best to try out for all the female characters. The experience of reading for the smaller parts would help me prepare to read for the bigger roles, or so I thought. Then if I did not get one of the major parts, I would still have an opportunity to take one of the lesser parts instead. I thought a small part was better than no part.

I did not anticipate what happened next. Once I read the first part, they gave it to me. They stopped the auditions; no one else even had an opportunity to try out. My fate was sealed with the first reading. Who would have imagined something like that would have happened? I certainly did not.

I tried to convince the directors to let me read for the other parts, but they refused. They said that I was perfect for *this* part, and *this* part was perfect for me, and no one else would do. Of all the parts I did *not* want to play it was this one, playing the role of a fortune teller? I though, you must be kidding. Nevertheless, it was the role I was forced to play in my senior class play. That was many years ago! However, the role could not have been further from my own true personality. It is our personality gift, or our motivational gift that defines who we are. It is a gift from God.

Why is it important to operate in one's own Motivational Gift?

The cast has been set, and the parts have been awarded. Each of us has a specific role or part to play in the body of Christ. I cannot do Mary's part and Mary cannot do mine. Why? Because each of us was created with the specific gifts and talents needed to fulfill our purpose. No one else will do quite like you. Paul was referring to the uniqueness of each individual member in the body and the significance of their gift to the body when he wrote, "And the eye cannot say to the hand, 'I have no need of you;' or again the head to the feet, 'I have no need of you.'" 1 Corinthians 12:21

So, what is a motivational gift and why is it important? The motivational gift is referred to as one's personality or lifestyle gift. It is also known as the grace gift for we could not earn it, it was given by God's grace. It makes us who we are in terms of our personality, and it motivates us to act or react based upon that gift. It is fundamental to who we are or at least to who we are to become (if we choose to cooperate with God) and it is a gift from God the Father.

You might be questioning the biblical basis to support this concept; I am so glad you asked the question!

1 Corinthians 12:6 *"There are varieties of effects, but the same God who works all things in all persons."*

The KJV says operations instead of effects. We operate in the ministry through our motivational gift. The parable of Jesus regarding the pounds relates to the motivational gifts.

> *"And he called ten of his own slaves and gave them ten minas, and said to them, 'Do business with this money until I come back.'* Luke 19:13 NAS

We are to do business; we are to operate in our calling and fulfill our purpose through the use of our motivational gift. We are called to go into the entire world and preach the gospel. We are to make disciples. That is our business, God has commissioned us to take what he has given us and do business with it until he returns.

What are we to do with the gift he has given? You will notice that unlike the parable of the talents, in this parable he gave only one pound to each person. There were ten pounds and ten servants, one apiece.

As we look deeply at this passage, it becomes clear that Jesus is not referring to the spiritual gifts, because the Holy Spirit can give several gifts or manifestations to each person, not just one. We also know that this parable cannot refer directly to the five-fold ministry gift. Some are called to fulfill that five-fold ministry in the church but not all.

Therefore, the only gift set left that qualifies in this parable is the motivational gifts given by God the Father. In this scripture, there are seven motivational gifts, but we have only one motivational gift that is dominant, although we will have all seven in part. Jesus was the only one that operated in all seven motivational gifts in their fullness. He was complete and perfect.

What did Jesus instruct us to do? Occupy, and utilize the gift you were given to do the work of the ministry, to overthrow the kingdom of Satan and establish the kingdom of Heaven.

10 "As each one has received <u>a special gift</u>, employ it in serving one another as good stewards of the manifold grace of God. 11Whoever speaks, is to do so as one who is speaking the utterances of God; whoever serves is to do so as one who is serving by the strength which God supplies; so that in all things God may be glorified through Jesus Christ, to whom belongs the glory and dominion forever and ever." Amen. **1 Peter 4:10-11**

The motivational gift is usually something we think of as the personality gift we were born with, but it is generally understood that it is not sanctified for the Father's use until we have been born again. The word sanctified means to be "holy or set apart". If you look at the word motivate you can see the root of two different words that have been put together, the words motion and action. Therefore, it is our motivational gift that causes us to move and act in the way that we do.

We presented in a previous chapter the numerous ways that we can be motivated. We discussed fear, incentive, character, or attitudes. We also learned that the members come together like the bones of the body. We come together at the joints which are right relationships, and they are supported by the ligaments which reflect right attitudes.

Let us look at this again for this is vitally important.

The bones, which we are as the members of the body, must come together at the joints. We do this through proper relationships with one another. The scripture tells us not to forsake the assembling of ourselves. It is important that the bones come together on a regular basis to foster good relationships. When we come together in love it is the bond of perfection which is the glue that holds the body together.

Those relationships create the integrity of the body. They are supported by ligaments which are good attitudes. When we each come together in the body of Christ, functioning in our right attitudes, it fosters the best possible union and fulfillment of function, strengthening the whole body.

How the Bones of the Body Are Fit Together

<u>Bones</u> are the individual members of the body.

They come together at the <u>joints</u> which are right relationships with one another.

They are supported by ligaments which are proper attitudes.

They are held together by the bond of peace in love.

Who fits the bones together in the right place?

The five–fold ministry is responsible for helping the individual bones find their place.

How do the bones minister to one another?

We minister through the gifts of the Holy Spirit.

We were each given a measure of the gift of Christ, and we become whole as we are joined together in love. The body of Christ needs our gift to be whole. The body cannot function fully or be complete until we discover our gift and minister through the gift of God which is our motivational gift.

For a better understanding of this concept, take time to look at the following scriptures. Study them, meditate on them, and ask God to reveal himself to you through them.

Ephesians 4:15, *"but speaking the truth in love, we are to grow up in all aspects into Him who is the head, that is, Christ"*

Colossians 2:19, *and not holding firmly to the head, from whom the entire body, being supplied and held together by the joints and ligaments, grows with a growth which is from God."*

Colossians 3:14-15, *"In addition to all these things put on love, which is the perfect bond of unity. ⁱ⁵ Let the peace of Christ, to which you were indeed called in one body, rule in your hearts; and be thankful."*

Ephesians 4:3, *"being diligent to keep the unity of the Spirit in the bond of peace"*

John 13:34-35, *I am giving you a new commandment, that you love one another; just as I have loved you, that you also love one another. ³⁵ By this all people will know that you are My disciples: if you have love for one another."*

How many motivational gifts are there?

There are seven gifts in all. They are Prophecy, Serving, Teaching, Exhortation, Giving Administration, and Mercy.

We each have one gift that is more dominant, but we have portions of all seven. Jesus who was perfect had all seven. We cannot attain this perfection without one another. We each have a measure or part which does not become complete except when we are joined together in Him.

Hindrances for discovery and use of your motivational gift:

- Personal behavior problems.
- Immaturity.
- Lack of Involvement with others in the body.
- Selfish and Carnal attitude.
- Failure to understand why certain ministries appeal to us.
- Sin

What is the purpose and benefit of ministering through your motivational gift?

Purpose – Fulfill the call of God upon your life.

Benefits –

- Personally, it makes us interdependent with one another.
- Brings the church into a greater level of maturity
- It organizes the church.
- It eliminates competition and frees each member to function fully when in their place.
- It brings peace, satisfaction, and fulfillment to each member individually and to the body corporately.

The Motivational Gift of Prophesy

To follow is a brief description of each gift, with their requisite strengths and weakness. Remember, this is a description of tendencies for each gift, it is not an indictment or a diagnosis.

People with the dominant gift of prophesy (also referred to as perceiving) can have strong opinions about right and wrong. Peter is one who exhibited many of the following tendencies. Remember these are merely tendencies often seen in people with this gift, but not necessarily a rule.

They understand God's heart and wish to defend it openly. They have an extraordinarily strong, uncompromising personality and can seem difficult to get along with at times. This is primarily due to their unwavering thoughts and beliefs. They know what is right in their own eyes and will not hesitate to tell you so. They tend to have strong feelings regarding their opinions and have a need to express those thoughts. It is therefore especially important for the prophetically motivated person to learn to speak the truth in love, having compassion.

There are times when they seem to have no tolerance for others' mistakes and find difficulty forgiving others. They tend to make snap judgments and are quick to correct and criticize others. When one remembers to extend the same grace that was given to us, we can avoid stepping over the line into a critical spirit.

They do have a very intuitive sense regarding how God sees things, a type of Holy Ghost sixth sense if you will. They can seem very extreme at times and tend to move past fact finding straight to the judgment portion of a decision without seeking counsel from others. They want to see quick action regarding wrong doings and tend to reject the person as a warning to others.

Presenting ideas with tact and giving people freedom to have their own opinions is incredibly important. One must give people the right to disagree even when we know (or at least strongly assume) that we are correct. They can be tenacious in their beliefs and once they take a stand, they are like bull dogs, holding fast to the stand they take. This can be either bad or good. It depends upon the spirit in which they present the view. They tend to be very persuasive when defining right from wrong and they desire to see repentance and change.

At times complex situations tend to be over simplified. Once again, we might attribute this to seeing things as either all black or all white with no gray areas in between. They become very broken when they fail. Peter is a striking example of just such a person. He was head strong and opinionated but loyal and eager to prove his commitment to Jesus. Therefore, when he denied Jesus the night he was arrested, he became distraught.

Once he overcame the brokenness, he was one of the strongest allies in the cause of fulfilling the Great Commission. His outspokenness was used for good on the day of Pentecost, resulting in many accepting the Lord.

Those with this dominant gift are willing to suffer for doing what is right because they are so deeply committed to the cause of justice and truth. Because of their intense sense of right and wrong they can sometimes have a very narrow, short-range view of circumstances. Maintaining an open mind can sometimes be a challenge for a prophetically motivated person.

It is especially important to remain aware of the negative tendencies, but one does not need to become discouraged by them. When we understand this motivational grace from God, we can work to overcome any apparent weakness and use them as strengths instead.

When they do not remain in the Spirit, they can have a tendency to exhibit the following characteristics:

- Hypocritical
- Rebellious
- Judgmental
- Insensitive
- Impatient
- Negative attitude
- Demanding of others
- Legalistic
- Critical

If I wanted a loyal follower that I can trust to watch my back, the person with this gift who has committed themselves to my cause would be the ideal candidate. Once they have made up their mind to support a person or cause, they would be hard pressed to turn back.

Because of the tendencies mentioned here, they are easily misunderstood and thought to be too harsh and frank. Others may view them as unyielding, headstrong, unfriendly, rude, and even manipulative. Sometimes their boldness can cause others to be afraid of them. Remember, without submission to the Holy Spirit these traits can all become very real. Walking in love and operating in the fruit of the spirit are extremely crucial, and required by the Lord, irrespective of one's gifting.

One of their most striking abilities is to be able to discern good from evil, while both exposing and confronting the evil. This is necessary to protect the church from those who wish to deceive. They are persuasive, authoritative, and courageous. Once again, this can be used to unite or divide depending upon how one uses their gift.

Having the motivational gift of prophesy does not make one a prophet, nor does it ensure that they will have the spiritual gift of prophesy. Each of these gifts operates independently of one another.

Others in the bible with this gift include Elijah, Jeremiah, John the Baptist, Isaiah, and Jonah (of course, all of these are clearly prophets).

The Motivational Gift of Serving

The person with this dominant motivational gift can be a great asset to the church and a loyal helper. They genuinely enjoy taking care of the practical needs of others and seek opportunities to do so, often doing more than what is expected or even needed at times.

They enjoy doing manual labor and will work alone if need be, to see a task completed. They enjoy working toward short term goals and prefer smaller projects, where quick results can be seen. Sometimes they will even use their own funds to see a project completed rather than wait to obtain the necessary funds through the appropriate channels. They like their instructions spelled out in detail.

This servant has a deep need to be accepted, needed, and verbally affirmed by those they serve. They often feel inadequate or unqualified for leadership roles. They are very sincere, caring, and loving people. They are both hospitable and generous. They do not like to delegate work to others, which can lead them toward the tendency to become overworked. They are highly energetic and tend toward perfectionism. They are meticulous about the work they do and dislike clutter. Their enthusiasm and ambitious standards can cause others to feel intimidated.

When they fail to walk in the Spirit, they can become vulnerable to:

- Overwork
- Self-pity
- Having a judgmental attitude
- Lack of direction
- Withdrawn
- Hurt
- Feeling unappreciated
- May become too pushy in desire to help others
- Can neglect family needs to meet needs of others

They do well as ushers, greeters, and on the hospitality committee. They are very resolute, sincere, and loyal people. They see life as a series of activities and their orientation is toward others.

Biblical examples can be found in Martha, Phoebe, Stephen, and Timothy.

The Motivational Gift of Teaching

Teachers love books, bookstores, research, maps, atlases, etcetera and enjoy systematic, logical, and sequential presentation of the facts. They love word studies and using research books such as concordances and dictionaries and insist on accuracy. This trait may seem unnecessary to others. Their preoccupation with details and facts may make them seem insensitive at times.

Teachers prefer teaching believers rather than doing evangelism. They are more objective than subjective. They prefer illustrations that are taken directly from the bible rather than from life experiences. They are very self-disciplined. They have a select group of friends and are emotionally self-controlled.

Their objectivity may make them seem cold and they appear to lack feeling at times. They enjoy using the Word to solve problems and they use an analytical approach to the truth. They are intellectually sharp and tend to develop a large vocabulary. This can lead to pride if they do not monitor this tendency and walk in humility.

They tend to focus on accuracy and truth and will have to investigate the teachings of others before accepting their teaching.

The teacher is vulnerable to being:

- Insensitive
- Proud and critical
- Impatient
- Wordy
- Dogmatic
- Inconsistent
- Impractical

Teachers can run the risk of becoming so fact oriented that they fail to focus on the application of the truth in their lives. They may neglect the needs of those they serve in favor of time to spend studying. They may become so dependent upon their study skills that they discredit the ability of the Holy Spirit to bring illumination and revelation in the word.

Once again, it becomes crucial that one know the areas in which they are vulnerable and take measures to prevent falling into those areas by remaining intimate with Holy Spirit daily.

Biblical examples are Ezra, Apollos, Luke, and Priscilla

The Motivational Gift of Exhortation

Those that have this gift are both motivators and encouragers. They are motivated to encourage people to enjoy the abundant life. They are overly optimistic and loving and tend to look on the positive side even in adverse situations. They like to stimulate the faith of others so that they can reach their full potential in Christ.

They can usually discern where people are spiritual and can minister to them at that level. They like to map out practical steps to help people grow and have no problem working with diverse groups of people. In fact, they like to encourage unity in believers from diverse groups.

They tend to view their trials and troubles as opportunities in which they can grow. They love people and enjoy helping them grow and mature. They are very patient and caring people; they do not give up easily. They usually make excellent counselors.

They like to begin with an experience then they apply the Word to meet the personal and practical needs. They take an experience and help the listener see a biblical truth embedded in the experience. They like to see the word applied to the will as well as to the mind and the emotions. They are unhappy if a message is not made practical and does not bring people to a decision. Their cheerful outlook and positive attitude may seem unrealistic at times and others may think they are overly confident and independent.

Exhorters may become vulnerable to:

- Rationalizing sin
- Oversimplification
- Presumption
- Allowing others to use them as a crutch
- Legalism
- Overconfidence
- Independence

Examples of biblical exhorters are Barnabus and Paul.

The Motivational Gift of Giving

This believer has a giving heart and a giving spirit. They are willing to share of their own money, material wealth, spiritual blessing, and personal time with others.

They have a knack for knowing how to make and manage their finances. They are good money managers and usually live well under their means. They are frequently wealthy and their wisdom regarding making and investing money far exceeds the everyday experience; it extends into divine purpose.

The giver likes to encourage others to invest in the kingdom and they are keenly aware of the financial needs of others. They are self-motivated when it comes to giving to meet needs and they need no encouragement to do so. They prefer to give anonymously.

They like it when their giving is an answer to someone else's prayer and prefer that the amount of the gift be confirmed in prayer by a spouse or business associate. They prefer to give in response to God's direct nudging and, not in response to an appeal.

I worked for someone who had this gift. In fact, he was exercising the gift at an early age. When I met him, it was in response to accepting a position in the nursing home he owned. He was thirty-two years of age when he purchased the nursing home. Even as a young man he was incredibly wise with money and how to make it.

He went on to build an assisted living facility and beyond that he built an exceptionally large Christian radio station. He was a fine Christian man who simply had the gift of giving and the wealth to prove it. Some people simply have this gift. He loved to give back to those he knew and loved. He gave to his community, church, and to God's work. God knows the ones he can trust to distribute His wealth.

Those with this gift are vulnerable to:

- Using money to control others
- Using money to control the church
- Overemphasis on material things
- Others viewing them as their source instead of God.
- They could use their enthusiasm for giving to pressure others to give.
- Impulsive, frugal, or stingy

These folks see life in terms of giving gifts and are very oriented toward the needs of others. They love to share and distribute the wealth.

Biblical examples of those with this gift are: Abraham, Solomon, Dorcas, and Luke.

The Motivational Gift of Administration

(Also known as the gift ruling or leadership)

Those with this gift are excellent organizers, administrators, and leaders. They love to coordinate the efforts of others to reach a common goal. They are motivated to assist the body of believers reach their goals and achieve the fulfillment of their ministry. They have the vision to see long range and know how to break down a massive project into short term goals. They know how to delegate appropriate tasks to others and motivate them to complete the tasks.

They strive to maintain unity in those they are leading. They will not assume responsibility to lead a group without being given the authority to do so, unless there is no other leader available. They can withstand a great deal of pressure and even tolerate the criticism of others if necessary to see a task completed. Once a project is finished, they begin to look for a new one to begin.

They prefer to leave the smaller details to others; they have the ability to see ahead to the long-term results of the completed project. The person with the gift of administration will usually write down their goals and develop a plan of action to complete those goals.

They experience great satisfaction in seeing a project reach completion. They are positive in their leadership style and know how to encourage and motivate others to do their best. They expect loyalty from the people they lead. They set deadlines for themselves and work hard to complete the work within that deadline. They have a great deal of zeal to see a project through to completion, even during difficult circumstances.

What is the person with this gift vulnerable to?

- Pride, legalism, and control
- Insensitivity
- Lack of patience with others who are less able
- Insecurity
- Callous and uncaring
- Task focused instead of ministry focused
- Failure to get rest and stay healthy because of zeal to accomplish a task
- Their high standards make others feel driven instead of led.
- Critical of others who are less organized
- Their zeal can cause them to forge ahead of God and the Holy Spirit to start a project.

Biblical examples are Nehemiah, Moses, Joseph, and David.

The Motivational Gift of Mercy

The one with the gift of mercy is full of compassion, understanding, and empathy for others; sensitive, emotional, sympathetic, and merciful. They possess the ability to feel what others are feeling (empathy) enabling them to minister to others needs spiritually as well as emotionally. They have a deep-seated need to comfort others who are in distress empathizing with them in their time of need.

People with this gift can often overlook the shortcomings and quirks of others, giving mercy even when it may not be deserved. They often attract hurting people to themselves. Their primary concern is the emotional and spiritual needs of those they minister to rather than the physical and practical needs.

Because these are extremely sensitive individuals, they are also easily hurt by others. Normally they avoid confrontation, but should they sense insincerity they can become bold and outspoken to protect those that are hurting.

They work well with others who possess this same gift. Repression of their feelings can lead to depression. They are excellent listeners and often make good counselors. They are very intuitive about things that can hurt others. These people often develop friendships or relationships with the people who have the gift of prophesy. The saying, "opposites attract" may apply here.

These sensitive people are vulnerable to:

- Depression
- Being partial
- Lead by emotion
- Avoiding confrontation even when needed
- Bitterness
- Their empathy for someone of the opposite sex can cause their motives to be misunderstood.
- Their sincerity may make them seem friendly but close relationships can be difficult for them.
- May choose to suppress feelings to be accepted by others.
- Their desire to be wanted can cause them to enter into co-dependent relationships.

These people are very comforting and caring people. They are very people oriented. Biblical examples include: The Good Samaritan, Dorcas, and John (the apostle).

Conclusion

In this work, I have attempted to introduce the reader to the characteristics of each gift while presenting some areas in which a person with this gift might be vulnerable. Anyone can be in danger if we fail to keep a right attitude and maintain a close relationship with the Lord. Not staying in close contact with him so that we can hear his voice or being insensitive to the leading of Holy Spirit can cause us to fall into error and misuse our gift. We are all vulnerable and need each other, but most of all we need to allow Holy Spirit to lead and guide us.

When we stay in the Spirit and close contact with the Lord, we can be assured of good success and a fulfilled life. When we minister in joy by using the motivational gift God gave us, we can feel satisfied and fulfilled in the work he has given us to do. Complete peace, joy and satisfaction are ours. It will also serve to strengthen our brothers and sisters as we take our proper place in the body of Christ. We need each other to be complete and whole. The body needs you, in your place, functioning in the way God intended for you to function. We need each other. How can the use of one's motivational gift help grow the church? See below.

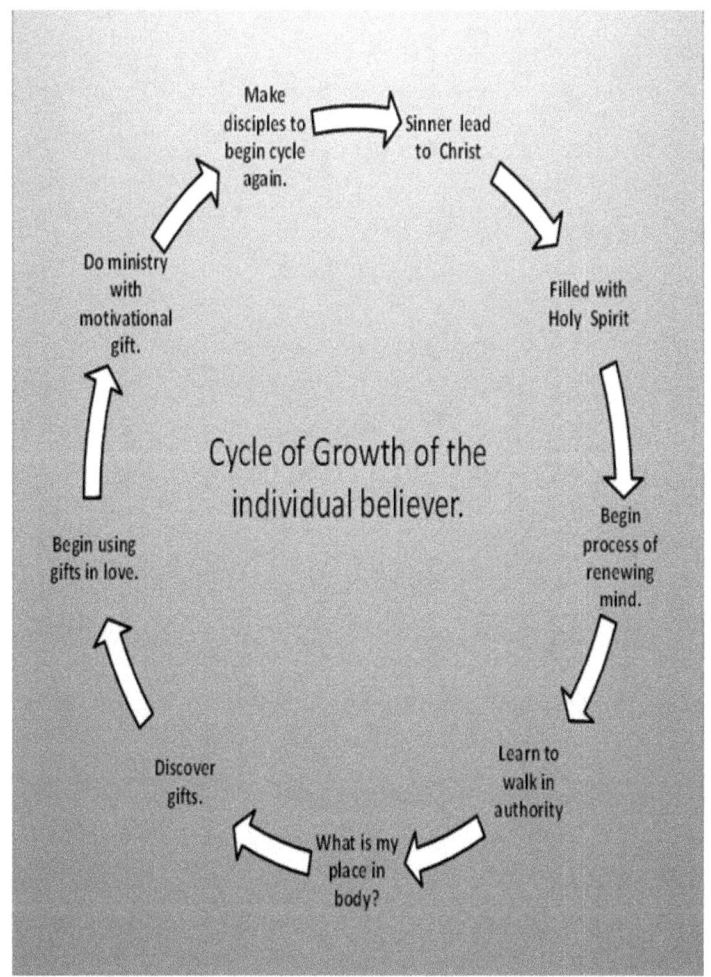

Chapter Ten:

Dry Bones to Glorified Bride

This book, from start to finish, has been about the preparation of a bride, the bride of Christ. It is a rag to riches story if you will, and it is also the story of a plan that went bad. Adam was living in paradise with a woman who was perfect and ageless; she was adorned with all that she needed…the glory of God. When Adam looked at her all he could see was the glory. He was to live forever in paradise with this beautiful bride… walking and talking with God. Man was complete and the two were one. So far it sounds like a beautiful plan.

Unfortunately, the story doesn't end there. We know that Satan could not leave Adam and Eve alone to live happily ever after, so he devised a plan of his own that included what some would say was an apple. We only know it was the fruit of a forbidden tree. Once the dastardly deed was completed and Adam and Eve had both partaken of the forbidden fruit, the glory lifted and they found themselves naked, dead in sin.

No longer could they walk and talk with God in the cool of the day. The scales formed on their eyes, and they were evicted from their home, paradise. God had clothed them with his glory, but once sin had entered the picture, they found themselves naked. They had been stripped of the glory and God's covering as well. Now they would need some clothing of their own to cover the sin.

Unfamiliar words were added to their vocabulary, the words were work and pain. It seemed that God's plan had fallen through, and the enemy had won; but wait, the story doesn't end there. God had another plan, he always does. He always knows how to take that which was meant for evil and turn it into good.

You see a hero arrived on the scene; his name was Jesus Christ. He cleansed man's sin with his own blood. No longer would they need the blood of goats and bulls. The price was paid in full, and it was good from that day forward, that is right; it was for all of eternity. Once man believed and received, the glory of God was his for the taking. The scales fell off and the work began, but the mind must be renewed. Off with the old and on with the new.

From glory to glory we stand gazing into the mirror. We find that we are being transformed to become the very one that we behold there, Jesus Christ. Once again, the glory fills the temple, and once again the glory fills the earth, one vessel at a time.

How does the bride of Christ, once dead in her sin, rise to take her place? How does she come together to form the army of the Lord? The first clue can be found in Ezekiel 37 where the bones are commanded to come together. Can the dry dead bones live again? We know that they can. So, he commanded them to come together, and they responded to the call. Forsake not the assembly of yourselves the bible says. And the closer the time comes the more we are to draw together to become one in him. So, the bones come together, and he covers them with flesh and skin.

Ezekiel was ordered to command the wind to blow upon them and it did, and they were filled with new life like new wineskins that had been filled with new wine. Like the dry bones we have been commanded to come together in newness of life and be endued with power from on high.

What does God require of you in your new life? Paul says in Romans 12:1 "... Present your bodies a living and holy sacrifice..." Not so that we can die on the cross for our sins, but so we might live in Him! Then what?

In verse two it tells us to "not be conformed to the world but be transformed by the renewing of your mind...." We are to be transformed as we continue to gaze in the mirror.... As we look and meditate upon the word of God it has the power to transform us into the very image of God. As we meditate upon His word day and night, we will become what he is.

Then what? Go to Ephesians 1:10 in the KJV" and you can see once again how we are to be gathered as one, all things in Christ." The NAS says we are to be summed up.

No matter which version you look at, we are to all come together in Christ. Then the fourth chapter of Ephesians and verse eleven speaks of the gift of the five-fold ministry. What is the purpose of this gift to the church? It is for the work of equipping the saints, to build up the body of Christ.

Just like a master builder laying his brick, one brick at a time, each one is sized up and chosen to fit precisely in the right spot. The joints join the bricks one to another to form a strong wall and eventually a whole building, all of them are laid upon a solid foundation, our foundation is Christ.

It is the job of the five-fold ministry to assemble the believers together like the mason does his bricks. They must arrange them, placing them in the proper order and in precisely the right spot. It goes on to say that once they have come together in the proper order, each joint will supply each need. As we learned, the joints are the relationships we make with one another. The bones come together at the joints and are further supported by the ligaments which are good attitudes.

Our motivational gifts support these relationships. Holy Spirit empower us to minister to one another through the supernatural gifts of the spirit. It is then that we meet each need in the body. We do so through the exercising of our gifts. We are not complete in ourselves, but we are complete in Him.

How long are we to do this? Verse thirteen tells us until we attain unity in the faith and a mature man, until we become perfect like Christ. Each of us have the measure of Christ, we possess a measure of the gift of Christ. As we fit our measures together, we become whole which is the perfect man he speaks about. We can then find the fullness of the gift in him, having no lack because each joint has supplied each need in the body.

We are to maintain these relationships in love and in the bond of peace which creates the unity that Jesus prayed for so that we might become one. It is as we gather together as one that we become the mighty army of God, fit for battle as in Ephesians 6:10

As we can readily see in Ephesians 5:21, Christ truly loves the church. He cleanses it, washes it, and presents it to himself as the glorious church without spot or wrinkle.

We are the body of Christ, a body of believers, a mighty army, and a glorious bride. It is this body constructed by him, equipped, and arrayed with glory and he is coming back for us. The gifts of the Trinity have been given to the church to prepare her for the groom. Like a bride preparing for her wedding day, we are to prepare for him, our groom.

We do not want to be like the five foolish virgins that were unprepared for the bridegroom's return. We want to be like the five wise bridesmaids who prepared, even though they had no idea when he would return. They just knew that he would, and they prepared for him. We too must prepare for his return. The bride must get ready, for her wedding day is upon her.

I was reminded recently of a word of prophesy about God being able to deliver what he promised to us in his word. This is the word in part:

"I am God almighty and beside me there is none other, I am the maker of heaven and earth and I tell you that I am able to deliver what I promised to give to you."

There were twelve spies that went into the land that day to survey the promise. Ten came back with a factual report but it was not the truth, for God's word is truth. They said that because of the giants they could not take possession of what had been given them.

Two came back with the truth, for God's word is truth, and they said it is all true what they said, but they said we are well able to possess what he promised. One was the facts, but the other was the truth. Jesus is truth."

God says he is well able to give you precisely what he promised you. He is the God Almighty and he is not limited by man's thought, concepts, or timelines.

He is God and he is well able to deliver what he promised you he would. Do not listen to man's report when it is contrary to the word of the Lord. The Lord is well able to give you all that he promised you he would.

We are to use all the gifts and graces he has provided to us to benefit the body. Like Esther preparing to meet the King, we have all that we need to prepare us; we simply need to use the gifts he has given and possess the land.

We have this treasure in our earthen vessels and jars of clay. It is your spiritual DNA, the gift of God. My sincere hope and prayer has been that somewhere along the way, somewhere along this journey, you too have discovered your treasure. As you have read through each page from the front to the back, you could see yourself peering back from the depths of the page in the description of the gifts that you possess in your earthen vessel.

As a little girl, I loved to read bedtime stories. Most little girls do. I liked to hear the stories of how the princess met her prince and they lived happily ever after. Most people will tell you to just get a grip, there is no such thing as a Prince Charming. There is no princess, and there is no such thing as a story book ending, at least not in real life .... where they all live happily ever after.

I am sorry, but I believe there is. There is a princess or a bride if you will, and there is a Prince Charming coming to gather her up, his name is Jesus Christ. Do you want to hear the best part of all? There is such a thing as a story book ending to life, because they do live happily ever after.

So, what is your gift, your motivational gift that is? And what gifts has the Holy Spirit given to you to minister with, do you know?

You may or may not be a part of the five-fold ministry, not everyone is. But you do have a specific dominate motivational gift, everyone does. We also know that Holy Spirit disperses gifts according to his will. We are told to desire the best gifts, but most of all; we are to desire to prophesy.

The entire world is waiting for the children of God to discover who they are. Its time you discovered your gift and used it to glorify him.

Where do you fit into the body?

Closing Thoughts

We have discussed many concepts in this primer on spiritual gifts, all from the aspect of discovering your gifts. We included a discussion on the anatomy of the church and the importance of ministering to the church body using your spiritual gifts given by Holy Spirit.

We do not want to be negligent of the days, times, and spiritual atmosphere in which we currently find ourselves living. Things are changing and very rapidly at that... and already we see many seeking God amid the chaos. Many would suggest we are already in the beginning of a massive end time harvest. We do not want to ignore the fact that many brand-new believers may soon be entering the church doors. New believers who may have never attended a church on a regular basis.

Our attention must include preparing for brand-new Christians getting filled with the spirit and stepping out with enthusiasm to exercise their newfound gifts. We need to be prepared to mentor and disciple brand-new believers helping them to not only discover their gifts but learn to use them within the safe environment of a loving, patient, and nurturing church family.

Just as our babies in the natural fell frequently when learning to walk, we must remember that new believers may not get it right the first time, the second time or even the third time they try. We encouraged our natural children to try again, we need to be just as understanding and supportive of our spiritual babies. There has never been a more exciting time to be alive and a part of God's church.

I trust the information you have learned in this book helps you to understand more fully the fabulous gifts God the Father, God the Son, and God the Holy Spirit provide to us. May you use the gifts entrusted to your care to bring God glory.

In closing, I must again echo the sentiments penned from the start:

"More than any day before, it is crucial that the church wake up, find her voice, and exercise her authority. Understanding your identity in Christ, discovering your gifts, and using them as God intended to benefit the body is your responsibility as a wise steward. We must each take responsibility to find our place and do our part to empower the church. This is arguably the most important day and hour in the history of the church, there is much at stake."

To God be the Glory,

Kathy

About the Author

Dr. Kathy Smith has a Doctoral Degree in Leadership from Vision International University and an Associate Degree in Nursing from Excelsior College. She is the Director of Curriculum Development and Communications at Vision International University, and an ordained minister with the Assemblies of God International Fellowship.

Formerly from Ohio and North Carolina, she lived in Ramona, CA from 2012 to 2018. In 2018 she relocated to Grand Blanc, Michigan and she continues to work for Vision International University remotely from Michigan.

As an author and educator, she travels to minister in local churches as the Lord leads. Her travels have taken her to the Dominican Republic, El Salvador, Austria, and Brazil.

She has authored the following books:

- Treasures of the Heart, The Gifts of the Trinity,
- Wisdom Speaks: Hearing Her Voice In A Noisy World,
- Effective Pastoral Care Ministry in the Local Church
- Healthcare Chaplaincy
- The Power of Unity, Empowered Believers Empower the Church
- Co-Authored: Develop a Pastoral Care Ministry in YOUR Church (combining the author's book Effective Pastoral Care Ministry with Dr. Stan DeKoven's book, 5 Steps to Effective Christian Counseling)

You may contact Kathy at ksmith.vision.edu@gmail.com or visit her website at www.kathysblog.org

There will be a Spiritual Gifts Study Guide and Spiritual Gifts tests available soon. Contact Vision Publishing for more details. www.booksbyvision.org

www.ingramcontent.com/pod-product-compliance
Lightning Source LLC
LaVergne TN
LVHW051840080426
835512LV00018B/2992